A LOVE UNRIVALED

A SEER'S VIEW

Then He said, "Hear now My words: If there is a prophet among you, I, the LORD, make Myself known to him in a vision; I speak to him in a dream" (Numbers 12:6)

PAT WORKS

All scripture is taken from the *New King James Version, Life Application Study Bible*, copyright © 1988. Used by permission of Tyndale House Publishers, Inc., Wheaton, IL 60189. All rights reserved.

Cover photo taken at Orange Beach, Alabama by James C. Works

Copyright © Pat Works 2012
All rights reserved.

ISBN: 1470002299
ISBN 13: 9781470002299

TO GOD BE THE GLORY

TABLE OF CONTENTS

Foreword 7
Acknowledgements 13
What Is a Seer? 17
Dreams, Visions and a Word 27
SECTION ONE: LOVE'S CALL 29
   A NEW BEGINNING 33
   HOLY SPIRIT ENCOUNTER 37
SECTION II: LOVE'S REVELATION 41
   Unconditional Love 45
   Love Never Fails 53
SECTION III: BORN ANEW IN CHRIST 57
   Set Free 61
   Dying to Self 69
   A New Creation 75
   Clothed With Christ 83
SECTION IV: CHRIST'S EXAMPLE 89
   The Open Door 93
   Love Your Brethren 101
   Jesus Is Our Example 111
   All That Glitters Is Not Gold 119
SECTION V: HOLY SPIRIT REVELATION 125
   Law vs. Spirit 129
   Prophetic Evangelism 141
   Encountering Stumbling Blocks 151
   Standing Strong in Faith 161
   In God's Strength 169

SECTION VI: WHEN CHRIST RETURNS............ 173
    The End Time Harvest..177
    The Wedding dance 185

SECTION VII: LOVE REVISITED 191
    Amazing Grace..195
    Love Unrivaled: Invitation................................. 205
    When the Night is Falling................................. 211
    Closing and Prayer...213
    Bibliography 215
    Second Chances: The Author's Story 217

♥ FOREWORD

Don't let the word *seer*, which you'll find in this book, throw you. The term describes those Christians who have been gifted by the Holy Spirit to see things more clearly than most of us. I should know; I'm married to one. The unsaved husband of a prophetic intercessor (another descriptive term for a seer) once told me, "Pastor, my wife is one of those intercessors. If I ever committed adultery, by the time I got home God would have told her who it was, what we did, and more. God tells my wife everything." It's true. God does reveal things to those with the unique gifts of discernment mentioned in Romans 12.

There have been countless times when my wife, Alice, would tell me something God told her in prayer, and within days, weeks, or months it was unfolding before our eyes exactly as she'd seen it. She and I have shared many of those experiences in the books we've written.

Pat Works is a wonderfully gifted Christian who heard me once say, "Whatever God gives us is on its way to someone else when we get it. Our job is to make sure they get it." A few years later she called and said she felt it was time to "pass on" what God had shown her. That's a bold move, a tremendous task, and it requires great humility.

One rarely has the opportunity to be mentored by someone like Pat. In this book she takes us "backstage" into her experiences with the Holy Spirit and offers us much-needed guidance and instruction. She clears up much of the confusion that exists in this area of Christian living.

We are not all prophetically gifted seers. But Jesus said that His sheep would hear His voice. We should all be growing to recognize His voice from among the many voices we hear. Pat, thank you for providing us with such clarity.

Friend, what you are holding is more than a book. It's a divine tool that, in the hands of the Holy Spirit, will help shape your life into the image of Christ. Grab a pen and pad. Take your time. Process each call to action you find scattered throughout this text. Like me, you too will find it transformative!

Eddie Smith

President and Cofounder
US Prayer Center, Houston, Texas

A LOVE UNRIVALED

"I am my beloved's and my beloved is mine"
(Song of Songs 6:3)

*You see, my brethren, my heart is full; I could almost say it is too big to speak,
and yet too big to be silent, without dropping a word to you.*
-George Whitefield, author

The Whitefield quoted herein was a very influential figure in the establishment of Methodism as well as he was an Anglican itinerant minister.

♥ ACKNOWLEDGEMENTS

I begin by thanking God for bringing me into the truth of all that He is, the reality of Christ Jesus as my Lord and Savior, and His Holy Spirit within me. If not for the revelation of His love, this book would not have been written, for it is about Him. Abba Father has led me to write it in order to share these revelations with you, the reader. He has guided me with His Word and presence. (He has never failed me.)

My husband Jimmy has been my biggest supporter in this effort. Without his love for me and his faith and confidence in my ability to accomplish this task I would have quit long ago. He patiently understood when I spent countless hours writing at the computer. Thank you, Jimmy. You are my best friend and the love of my life.

I have two dear sisters in Christ, Kami Lockett and Sondra Hill, who made a commitment to pray without ceasing as I began the task of writing this book. Their consistency in prayer, as well as checking on me and spurring me on, allowed me to keep to the task with a single purpose: Finish what God called me to do. I liken them to the biblical story of Aaron and Hur in the chapter 17 of Exodus. As Joshua fought the battle against Amalek, Moses held his hands up to the heavens. As long as Moses' hands were held high, Joshua won the battle. When Moses grew tired, he sat down on a rock, and Aaron and Hur came alongside him. With one on each side, they held up Moses' arms. Thus, Joshua continued to fight, and he won the battle with Amalek (Exodus 17:12). Just as Aaron and Hur came alongside Moses, Kami and Sondra came alongside me and refused to let me give up. Through their faithfulness in prayer, they made sure I was seated on the "Rock" of Christ. Thank you, Kami and Sondra. Without your prayers, I would have fallen by the wayside long ago. You are special to me.

To my prayer partners and intercessors: I know each one of you personally. I am confident your avid prayers, with unceasing love, are always there for me. It is in knowing that you are faithful that I receive strength and courage to push through. You are a blessing to me.

To my family: From birth, every circumstance of my life has shaped me. I began with family. Good or bad, perfect or imperfect, each family member has played a part in how I was nurtured and reached adulthood. Of course, my mother played a large part in my life in many ways. She was the one who held my feet to the fire to attend church. Her rule was, "No church, no going out!" I wasn't about to miss going out, so I dutifully attended church. In the process of what I thought was an abiding of church only, I learned of the reality of God and of Christ's sacrifice. Throughout my baby years to adulthood, I had no idea how much I would rely on these truths later in life. I give credit to my mother for the sure foundation that I would much later come to understand in a deeper sense. Thank you, Mom. I love you.

To Billie Akers: If not for Billie's reading, editing, and close perusal of what is written herein, my ignorance in grammar and style would be blatantly revealed. Thank you, Billie, for your knowledge and finesse in adding the finishing touches to what I've written. You have allowed this book to make better sense to the readers as well as kept many English teachers from grinding their teeth. Thank you for your honesty and forthrightness in making corrections and suggestions. I am indebted to you.

To Eddie Smith, my writing mentor: Eddie is president and cofounder of the US Prayer Center in Houston. I am grateful to Eddie for his expertise, counseling, and mentoring as I labored over this book. It was only with Eddie's help that there is a finished product. Having met Eddie some years ago, I remembered that he offered his services as a coach to help people who write or desire to write. I contacted Eddie, and the book speaks for itself. His suggestions, tips, and telephone conferences were needed and greatly valued. Thank you, Eddie, for your patience and understanding of my apparent lack of knowledge.

We need a baptism of clear seeing. We desperately need seers who can see through the mist—Christian leaders with prophetic vision. Unless they come soon it will be too late for this generation. And if they do come we will no doubt crucify a few of them in the name of our worldly orthodoxy.
—A. W. Tozer, author

♥ WHAT IS A SEER?

The subtitle of my book is *A Seer's View*. I suspect that the word *seer* may be as foreign to you as it was to me when I first heard it. A seer is simply someone who sees what God is revealing to them in a dream, vision, or in His Word. My first encounter with the concept of a seer took place at a conference in which I was a member of a prayer team. One of the pastors attending the conference walked up to me with two other people and said, "You're a seer. These two people need prayer."

As he walked away, I was puzzled that he had referred to me as "a seer." However, I put that on the back burner and turned my attention to the couple before me. I did not ask them to tell me their prayer need but proceeded to allow the Spirit of God to lead me. After I sensed God speaking to me I began to pray what I was seeing in the spirit. At the ending of prayer, the couple told me that I had "hit the nail on the head." In other words, I *saw* their need and prayed accordingly. Once I was home I began to search out the word *seer* and found it referenced twenty-two times in the King James Bible. If you would like to further your own understanding of the seer gift, an excellent resource is *The Seer* by Jim W. Goll, cofounder of Encounters Network in Franklin, Tennessee. This book helped my understanding of the seer gift and calling. Goll writes:

> When it comes to prophetic revelation, a prophet is primarily an inspired hearer and then speaker while a *seer* is primarily visual. In other words the prophet is the *communicative* dimension and the seer is the *receptive* dimension. . . . The first lays emphasis on a prophet's relationship with the people; the second, on a prophet's revelatory relationship with God. . . .
>
> A prophet may have a particular grace to hear and proclaim the word of the Lord and yet not necessarily function as profusely in the revelatory visionary capacity as a seer does. The seer, on the other hand, may move quite remarkably in this visionary dream capacity yet not be as deep in the inspirational audible graces of hearing and speaking.

> Nevertheless, both move and operate in the prophetic realm, but in different capacities. (pp. 22-23)

The Old Testament prophet Samuel was a seer. Other seers mentioned in the Bible are Ado, the priest; Gad, David's seer; Iddo; Hanani; Asaph; Jeduthun; and Amos.

A seer was not uncommon in biblical days. Like all of God's gifts, that of the seer is relevant today. The problem lies in lack of knowledge and understanding of God's gifts. Scripture states that all who come to the knowledge of Christ are given gifts according to the Holy Spirit. Chapter 12 of 1 Corinthians gives us the knowledge and understanding of all the gifts given by the Spirit:

> But the manifestation of the Spirit is given to each one for the profit [of all]: for to one is given the word of wisdom through the Spirit, to another the word of knowledge through the same Spirit, to another faith by the same Spirit, to another gifts of healings by the same Spirit, to another the working of miracles, to another prophecy, to another discerning of spirits, to another different kinds of tongues, to another the interpretation of tongues. But one and the same Spirit works all these things, distributing to each one individually as He wills.

I found that not only did I see pictures or a word during prayer times, but that my dreams began to take shape as vivid stories—almost book length. I sometimes have short dreams and sometimes one-picture dreams, but mostly I dream at length. After some time, I began to see a common thread in many of my dreams. That was God's love. God wants us to know His love. As you read about the dreams in the following chapters, I pray that God draws you into an intimate union with Himself.

This brings me to another source that enhanced my understanding of God's love and the intimacy He wants with me. Although I had been saved for twenty-five years, I was unaware that there was a relationship of intimacy that I could have with God. His love is something that He wants you to know as well: the deep intimate love that He has for you. One of the best descriptions I've read on intimacy with God is found in Alice Smith's book *Beyond the Veil*. Smith describes the intimacy and love relationship God desires for each of us.

Friend, you can have as much of God as you want. Are you willing to invest your time and your tears? Will you let anything stop you from this deeper intimacy? Do you long to know the joy of abiding in Him?

He is waiting to commune with you (see Rev. 3:20). If you are hungry and thirsty enough, you will experience the fulfillment of Jesus' promise to all who seek, "Whoever believes in me, as the Scripture has said, streams of living water will flow from within him" (John 7:38). (Page 182).

I mention these two books, *The Seer* and *Beyond the Veil*, because this book, *A Love Unrivaled* is about the love of God that's been shown to me through the seer calling. They are one and the same to me: God's love revealed in dreams and visions.

For clarification, dreams and visions are not the only way God speaks His children. These are just some of the ways. God also speaks through His Word, by His Spirit to your spirit man, or through another person. It just happens that many times He has chosen to use dreams to speak to me or to bring revelation to a situation.

There are often truths revealed in a dream that may be for an individual but are also helpful for the church at large. Even though I am the one who has had a dream, often truths revealed in that dream can benefit other believers as well. I have found many times, as I shared a dream with others, there was always someone who received the dream and its interpretation for their current life's situation. In the same way, Paul, Peter, and James were writing to the early church, yet their writings still apply in our lives today.

Some caution with regard to dreams:
1. **Not all dreams are of God.** Just because you have a dream does not necessarily mean God is speaking something profound to you. Many times the circumstances of your day, what you ate, or difficult issues you are facing can cause what I would call an abstract dream. It is all mixed up and seems to make no sense. I always record my dreams, either rising in the night to write it down while it is fresh in my mind or

early in the morning. I have always found more clarity and interpretation in a dream when I begin to write it out. There are times when I immediately know what God is showing me and just as many times when I don't have a clue. These I pray over and wait on God's revelation. It may be a few days, weeks, or even years before the revelation is given. It is important to wait and trust that God's timing is always right. One should never get upset or hung up on trying to interpret a dream. If it is from God, God will give the interpretation, the application, as well as the timing for it.

2. **Mistakes are made when interpreting dreams.** It is vital that you seek God for all interpretations of dreams as well as what He would have you do with them. There have been times when people become so overwhelmed with a dream that they rush to tell the others in the dream, giving their own interpretation of it. Likewise, there are just as many people who seek another person's word instead of God's. God's revelation is the first you should seek. A question to ask is, Does the dream or interpretation line up with the Word of God? God's Word will confirm what He has given.

3. **What about when you receive a word from someone who had a dream and it never comes to pass?** Don't let a word given to you cause you to be anxious for its fulfillment. Trust God. If you put all your faith in someone's word you are likely to be disappointed. Go to God's Word and find out if the word given to you by man aligns with His. Seek God in the matter and set it aside. There are self-appointed prophets or seers giving words left and right to people. Much of the time their words fail to become a reality. My personal practice is to take a word someone speaks to me and give it to God. Letting it go for His perusal is vital. If the word is a true word, God will confirm it to you in another way. However, I have found in my life that most of the time a person's word confirms what God has already shown me. I could wallpaper my house with words people have spoken over me that have not come to pass. Does this mean they are false prophets? Not necessarily. It may mean that the word is not yet in God's timing. Remember, God told the Israelites they would be in bondage for four hundred years, and then He would bring them out of captivity. Don't

you think that at some point they began to lose hope and decide that deliverance would never come? God's timing is critical to your faith. Then again, delayed fruition of a word may mean the person missed it totally. The key is to look to God for the answers in your life. Take man's word, give it to God, pray over it, and set it aside.

4. **Know God's Word.** Be strong in the Word of God before receiving the word of man. If you are not familiar with God's Word, how then can you know when a word is true or false? Read His Word and let it become your guide to any other word you receive. You may be thinking that you cannot remember all of God's Word. Read it anyway. You will be surprised at what the Holy Spirit will do with God's Word once it is read. "But the Helper, the Holy Spirit, whom the Father will send in My name, He will teach you all things, and bring to your remembrance all things that I said to you" (John 14:26). Read God's Word, and the Holy Spirit will call it to your mind at the time that it is needed.

5. **Not all dreams are to be shared.** If you have a dream about someone, only as God leads is the dream or word to be shared with that person or even the church. For example, I had a dream about a young woman who I knew was having marital problems. As I did not sense God's leading to tell her the dream, I committed this couple to prayer. After a few weeks she called, and I felt led to tell her the dream and that I had been praying for them. She said that they had been having severe problems but a few days prior to her call to me, she and her husband had decided to seek counseling for their marriage. She was able to see God's love in that He had someone praying for them during this time frame. The purpose of the delay in revealing the dream was so that God's care and love would be revealed to this woman and not me or my prayers. I saw. I prayed. God worked. God received the glory.

6. **Dreams can be a blessing or a disappointment.** Whether a dream is given to you for personal reasons or for others, it can be a great blessing. For example, perhaps your church has been praying for revival and God reveals to you through a dream that revival is about to break loose. What a blessing of hope and encouragement that would be to the members to know this as they continue to pray. On the other hand, if you do not wait for God to interpret the dream but jump to

your own conclusions, then you might give an incorrect interpretation to believers that never comes to pass. This places you in the position of accountability for what you said, good or bad. If God gives the dream, God will give the interpretation. You must allow God to be the voice behind the revelation, interpretation, and application of every dream. You should be willing to set yourself aside and wait on God's timing for all things.

7. **Warning dreams:** Many dreams will give warning of something that is going to happen in your life. In this case, get into God's Word and go to prayer seeking God's will and purposes as well as further clarification. Prayer is always beneficial in any situation. Waiting upon God is a must.

Like you, I am a sinner saved by the grace. I am one whom God has chosen to reveal things through dreams and visions. However, whether you are a dreamer or not, you also hear from God. In this book I share some dreams that reveal the depths of God's love, growing up into Christ, being clothed with Christ, and much more. I invite you to read and receive these truths. They are for you. As you read, I pray that you will fully understand God's love and begin to experience the intimate relationship that He wants to have with you.

It is my prayer that through the revelation of God's love, as revealed in this book, you will find yourself plunged into a deeper love than you ever imagined. May our Holy God be revealed to you intimately, invading your heart, so that you may see Him in all of His beauty, light, and truth. Allow every chapter to bring you into further revelation of the lengths our Lord and God will go to in order for you to know His love.

Dreams and visions are one of the ways God speaks to me, reveals Himself, and helps me understand His truth. However, as I said before, it is not the only way God speaks. It just so happens that God chose dreams and visions to teach and assure me of His love.

If you are not a dreamer, please don't think this book is not for you. God has given gifts to each person who embraces Jesus as Messiah, and He does not give anyone gifts or talents to sit on a shelf. In fact, God is not pleased when you do not use your gifts, as Jesus told in parable of the talents (Matthew 25:14-30). God's gifts are to be used to enhance as well as equip the body of Christ. More importantly, they are to glorify Him. The gifts you have been given are to bring you deeper into His truth, as you speak the truth in love that you may grow up in all things into Him who is the head—Christ (Ephesians 4:15).

The gift I have been given is reflected in this book. I pray that it is multiplied by bringing you into a deeper understanding of God's love and that our Lord Jesus is glorified in and through you. This book is for everyone who desires to be loved by a love that is unrivaled and unconditional. If you want to experience this ultimate Love, you can.

Revelation is the activity of God by which He unveils or discloses or makes known what is, to humanity, otherwise unknowable. It is God making Himself known to those shaped in His image. Revelation is what God does, not what mankind achieves. It is a divinely initiated disclosure, not an effort or endeavor or achievement on the part of mankind.
Author: Sam Storms

♥ DREAMS, VISIONS AND A WORD

You will note that I placed the dreams contained in this book in sections as well as chapters. As I completed this writing and began to arrange the dreams, the Lord revealed a pattern to me. The first section is the beginning of my receiving these dreams, I then began to see that my dreams were of the Father, the Son and the Holy Spirit – the Trinity of God - as well as the second coming of Christ. Therefore, I used sections to separate the dreams as they relate to each person of the Trinity.

What is written in the dreams, visions, and words that follow are meant to shake you loose from one of the deadliest entities known to man—yourself! It is Satan's prideful and arrogant view of himself that caused him to be cast out of God's presence. Pride was his ruling emotion, and all else paled in comparison to it. God's Word warns repeatedly of rebellion and pride with reference to Satan as our example. Somehow many have come to think of Satan as either a figure of speech or even more horrifically (as well as dangerously), a fairy tale.

This book points to our Almighty, Sovereign, and Holy God's love for you. His Abba Father's heart is as Paul reminds us in the book of Galatians 4:6: "And because you are sons, God has sent forth the Spirit of His Son into your hearts, crying out, "Abba, Father!" (Galatians 4:6.

Father God longs for you to know Him intimately and have the understanding and revelation of who He is as well as who Christ is in you. I pray that the Holy Spirit will awaken your heart and open your spiritual eyes and ears to the sacrifice of love your Abba Father paid for you. When you enter into the reality of His love, you will be able to walk with boldness and confidence with a sure foundation. Beyond any doubt, you will know He is always there to catch you when you fall, forgive you when you ask, point you in the right direction when you waver, and chasten you in love when needed. "God is love" (1 John 4:8, 16). "Love never fails" (1 Corinthians 13:8).

Enjoy your journey with the Love of your life.

Note: For clarity, with each dream, vision, or word, I will state what it is, i.e., "Dream." I will then follow with "Truth" as the interpretation that has been revealed to me.

SECTION ONE
LOVE'S CALL

*Revivals begin with God's own people; the Holy Spirit
touches their heart anew, and gives them new fervor and compassion,
and zeal, new light and life, and when He has thus come to you,
He next goes forth to the valley of dry bones...
Oh, what responsibility this lays on the Church of God!
If you grieve Him away from yourselves, or hinder His visit,
then the poor perishing world suffers sorely!
Author: Andrew Bonar*

CHAPTER 1

♥ A NEW BEGINNING

In the fall of 1998, my husband Jimmy and I were living in southern Louisiana, having moved there from northern Louisiana in the summer of 1996. I grew up in the area so I was at home and around my family. My husband, a long-time (twenty-six years) insurance adjuster and then agent, decided to step out and try a new vocation, real estate. This was the reason for our move. He was presented with one of those "offers you could not refuse," and we went for it. Have you ever been given one of those offers? Well, as you will read later, it is true that "all that glitters is not necessarily gold."

When we sold both our home as well as our camp on the river within two weeks, we thought, "This must be God!" You have probably thought this in some particular circumstance in your life as well. Jimmy had been given what appeared to be a golden opportunity to be part of a small real estate office with just the owner and one other agent. Just step in, learn the nuts and bolts, and that's all there is to it. Or so we thought. God had other plans. Three months after our move, the owner died of a massive heart attack. His wife closed the real estate office, and Jimmy was left for the first time in his life without employment. Our house in northern Louisiana had been sold. Living in a rental home with most of our belongings still in boxes, we found ourselves in an extremely difficult place. Was this God or not? What happened? These were some of the questions we voiced numerous times. This was undoubtedly one of the times in my life that I hung on by a thread. I trusted God, prayed constantly, and tried to encourage my husband.

Because of my experience as a legal secretary, I was able to find employment right away. Knowing how hard it was for a real estate agent to make a living on commission alone, especially a new agent, Jimmy looked in other fields only to have the door shut in his face over and over. He settled for working in another real estate agency with many agents and three or four bosses. Although he continued to look for a position in other fields, it just didn't happen. Did I mention we were in a hard place? Every door was shut and there was "no room in the inn." After two and a half years in that area and our spirits still unsettled, we entertained the idea to move once again. I knew I could work anywhere. My greatest concern was for Jimmy to find employment that was fulfilling. We made the decision to move. It was November of 1998, and I had a dream.

*The Holy Spirit is the gift of the Risen Christ. His anointing filling, empowering
work is a baptism of love that gives power to make Jesus
real to you and known to others.*
Winkie Pratney, author

CHAPTER 2

♥ HOLY SPIRIT ENCOUNTER

Dream: Jimmy and I were walking down a road looking for a house to purchase. We looked to our left where there were some new houses. We stood admiring them. They were all built on a hill with a wooded area around them. It was quite picturesque. As we were commenting on how nice the houses were, one by one the houses began to slide down the hill in a mudslide. We were shocked and both agreed that it was a good thing we saw that before buying a house in that area.

We continued to walk down the road where we came to a large open field. It had the appearance of a field ready to be planted. We noticed a wide path that cut through the middle of the field to the other side. We decided to cross the field. As we started across, we noticed an old barn to our left. It was unpainted, decaying, and missing part of the roof as well as some of its side boards. We wanted to look in the barn so we entered it. As we were looking around, all of a sudden I shouted, "Get out! It's going to fall in on us and trap us here." Just as we got outside the barn collapsed. Once again we were grateful to have been spared the consequences of making a wrong decision.

We continued to walk across to the other side of the field. Arriving at the other side, we noted there was a fence across the land. We seemed to be at a standstill. We both turned and looked back over the field wondering where to go next. At this point, I looked up to my right and saw far in the sky a ball of bright light that appeared to be coming straight toward us. We both ducked as the ball whizzed past between us. I watched as the ball traveled back up in the sky, turned, and started back toward us again. All of a sudden I said, "Don't duck. It's the Holy Spirit." I stood firm as the ball of light came again and hit me full in the chest. Wham! It then flew out of my back. Jimmy ducked. The ball of light went back up again and twice more hit me in the chest going out my back. This happened three times in all.

Truth: "I will instruct you and teach you in the way you should go. I will guide you with My eye" (Psalm 32:8).

God promises to instruct us, teach us, and guide us in our path. He further promises to guide His children with His eye. How? Through His Word revealed to your spirit and through pictures, dreams, and visions that He gives to help you walk and stay on your path.

Jimmy and I never bought a house in southern Louisiana. That was not God's intention for us. In the dream, we were in Louisiana. Some of the houses in that area were like houses not built on a solid foundation. For God's will and purposes, this area was not a sure foundation for us. (This does not mean that this area is a bad area. It only means that for us, we were to move on as God led us. Only as we are in God's will do we stand on a sure foundation.)

The barn represented the old and the past, which sought to keep us out of God's will. It also represented the pull of family ties, as that was my birth place and my youngest son and grandchildren were there. However, God had other plans for us. The open field represented God's calling to come because there was much work to do and other areas for us to work.

As for the ball of light, I did not understand until later that this was an anointing by the Holy Spirit preparing me for the work that I would encounter in the very near future.

At the end of January 1999, we moved to the Birmingham, Alabama, area. After one week in town, I went to work for a large law firm. Jimmy found employment in sales. God had prepared us by not allowing us to stay in the area where we initially moved. Was it God who moved us to south Louisiana to begin with? I say, yes, it was. Jimmy says, no, it wasn't. Knowing my husband as I do, I felt God had to move him slowly to get him where He wanted him to be later. I don't know the absolutes of why we had to move from one end of Louisiana to the other to get to Alabama. I do know God was in control—that it was God who prepared us for the next move through the dream and revealed to us that the area where we were was not His final destination for us.

After two months on my new job in Alabama, God told me to start a Bible study. I say God "told me," and I want to clarify this. No, I did not hear an audible voice, but sensed a "still small voice" in my spirit (see 1 Kings 19:12). Today, when I hear this voice, I know it is God. There is no doubt in my mind. It is something that you know and do not doubt. There are times you may sense that you should do one thing or another but aren't sure. When God speaks, you know it is Him.

Starting a Bible study at work was not something I wanted to do. I had taught children in Sunday school, not adults, and my confidence level was not very high. However, as I knew it was God's voice I obeyed Him. I sent an email around to the secretaries inquiring if anyone was interested in a lunch-hour Bible study. To my surprise, I was flooded with many affirmatives. Until the day I retired on December 22, 2010, I taught either a weekly Bible study or held a prayer meeting during the lunch hour. I also developed an email ministry, which included friends I knew or worked with as well as some, to this day, I've never met and have only corresponded with by email. I spent twelve years at secular work and twelve years in spiritual work/ministry. I have learned over the years that our workplace is our ministry. Wherever you find yourself, you are to be the Lord's light of truth to those around you. It is the light of Christ within as well as your behavior that attracts others to Christ.

The Holy Spirit encounter in the dream was an anointing of preparation for teaching and leading Bible studies as well as ministry opportunities that began to come later. Over the years, God has done many works in me through dreams. This may sound unbelievable to the average person, but it is the way He has chosen to speak as well as prepare me for things to come.

When you are saved, you receive God's Holy Spirit. However, as you grow spiritually in your journey with Christ Jesus, there can be an added filling or anointing by the Holy Spirit for specific tasks. When I started to work at the law firm in Birmingham, I had a boldness and assurance I did not have before. That was God. That's what God wants to do in you. Do you reflect our Lord Jesus? Do people want to be around you? Do they come to you for prayer, a word or answer, for mentoring? Are you multiplying the talent God has given you? These are just some of the questions on which to reflect. Better yet, ask God, for He delights in answering His children.

On the cover of Smith Wigglesworth's devotional is this statement: "God is more eager to answer than we are to ask." Have you asked God where you are to be or what you are to be doing? Whether you work out of the home or in, you work. Your work place is the field in which He has ordained you to be in your daily life. You are to be the hands, feet, and heart of Christ Jesus in that place. Think about it. The chances are that most of you are working an eight-hour day with a lunch hour. You are spending nine hours of your day around people other than family. Are you representing Jesus?

If you find yourself in a workplace where you are not happy, ask God to move you. If He does not, settle down with full confidence and assurance that this is His will for you at this time. If God wants to move you, He will. Our Lord Jesus did not sit around with friends who thought like Him, acted like Him, spoke like Him. He did not have one person around Him who knew or understood Him. Yet He loved them all. He continued in His calling with His eyes and heart focused on one thing—His obedience to God! Are we not to do the same? "I delight to do thy will, O my God" was Jesus's heart (Psalm 40:8).

What about you?

1. Have you had an unusual Holy Spirit encounter? Have you shared it with others that they might be encouraged?
2. Are you following the Holy Spirit's leading or have you stopped and found yourself stagnated? What will you do to move forward?
3. Are you being Jesus to those around you, at home, work, or in the market place? If not, what will you do to allow Jesus to be seen in you?

SECTION II
LOVE'S REVELATION

Here is a spiritual principle: We cannot exercise love unless we are experiencing grace. You cannot truly love others unless you are convinced that God's love for you is unconditional, based solely on the merit of Christ, not on your performance. Our love, either to God or to others, can only be a response to His love for us.
—Jerry Bridges, author

CHAPTER 3

♥ UNCONDITIONAL LOVE

I will run the course of your commandments, for you shall enlarge my heart. (Psalm 119:32)

I was twelve years old and sitting in God's lap. Does that sound like a dream? It's the place you would like to find yourself—in God's lap. Actually, although it wasn't a dream, it was a vision I had in the spring of 2004. I was deep in prayer one day when I was taken into a vision. In this kind of vision, I was not asleep but was in fact watching myself in the vision.

Vision: I saw myself standing before God. I didn't see God's face, for no one can see God's face and live (Exodus 33:20). But in my spirit I knew it was God. I seemed to be around twelve years of age. (For some reason, many times God takes me back to being twelve years old, as you will see in some of the dreams that follow. I think it has to do with the "come as a child" command Jesus stated in order that I see, hear, and trust rightly and not lean toward that of my older, opinionated mind-set.) Here I saw myself in front of God. He motioned with His hand for me to come forward, as He spoke, "Come here." With trembling and fear, I stepped forward and God lifted me into His lap, sitting me on His left knee with His left arm around me. God spoke again saying, "You're afraid of me, aren't you?" I was speechless. I slightly nodded my head in the affirmative with eyes as big a saucers. God said, "I love you. You are my daughter. And I will never be angry with you." He then pulled me to Himself, hugged me, and set me down on the ground (or was it the clouds?). He turned me around to go forward from Him and swatted my bottom as you would a child. He said laughingly, "Now, go play!" I stepped forward a few steps and turned around and looked at God, my mind questioning silently, "Play?" Then, although I did not speak aloud, God answered, "My work is play, if you do it right," and He smiled at me.

Now thus far, this dream would be enough for most people. Sitting in God's lap—wow! But not for me. I had to "go the extra mile."

Still in the vision, I stood there questioning if it could be true that God would never be angry with me. (Keep in mind that I'm watching this scene unfold before me.) I saw myself step up to God and stomp on His left foot and step back. That's right! I stomped hard on God's foot and stepped back from Him to see what He would do. (Testing God is something we are commanded *not* to do, but this was a bit much.) So, in the natural, I was literally horrified as I watched myself do this. My mind was saying, "I wouldn't do that, God." Yet, there it was right in front of me. I stomped on the Creator of the universe, God Almighty's foot. God looked at me and once again motioned for me to come forward. This time with way more fear and trembling, I cautiously stepped up, expecting to be spanked, punished, something, for my actions. Instead, He picked me up, set me back on His knee with His arm once again around me, and said, "You thought I was going to be mad at you, didn't you?" With much apprehension, I nodded my head. "I told you that I would never be angry with you. I love you. Do you know what makes me angry?" He asked. I shook my head no as he replied. "When people hurt other people, that angers me." Still in the vision, as I gazed at my Father God, I reached within myself and took out my heart (a very small thing) and lifted it with both hands, offering it to God. He smiled and received it from me. However, in return, He handed me His heart. As I held His heart in my hands, I said, "But God, Yours is so much bigger than mine." He simply smiled and said, "Yes, but I'm making yours like Mine."

Truth: "For this is like the waters of Noah to Me; for as I have sworn that the waters of Noah would no longer cover the earth, so have I sworn that I would not be angry with you, nor rebuke you" (Psalm 54:9).

I have heard it taught that dreams are symbolic and visions are literal. This caused me to be in awe of what I had just been shown. Could it be true? God would never be angry with me? God gave me His heart. God loves me? Then the old doubt slipped in, and I began to question if the vision was real. I found out quickly in the next few days. I noticed that I walked with a new step. I wasn't afraid anymore that if I messed up God would be angry at me. I was able to see quickly when I failed and would confess and repent and go on in the beautiful love of my Father God. I noticed I began to love people more than I had before. In that vision, God did a work within me by His Spirit assuring, as well as cementing within me, His unending love for me. He loosed me from the bondage of conditional love, something that was instilled in me from a young child.

The ultimate beauty of this vision is that God has shown me that this is a reality for you and all others who are bound by conditional love. If you will accept the vision for yourself, you too will be loosed to receive His heart and walk in unconditional love. Father God's heart. His love. What more could you ask?

How many of us grew up with conditional love? You know what I'm talking about. If you are good, you are loved. If you are bad, you are not loved anymore. You lived in fear when your parents were angry and felt as if you were locked in a dark closet somewhere waiting to be released. And so you were. Your spirit thrives on love. God created us to love and be loved. When parents are angry, they don't verbally say they don't love you anymore, but somehow their attitude carries that nonverbal insinuation. A parent's anger or disapproval comes across clearly and has great effect on a child. It can carry far into their adult years, affecting every choice they make. You were rewarded with smiles when you obeyed. You might have found yourself compared to a sibling or even someone else's child who seemed to be the picture of perfection. The comparison made your mistakes look larger than ever. If you missed the mark, then what followed was the frown, the scolding, the visual disappointment, and most of all, the anger. You felt your parent's love had been snatched completely away from you. I am not saying all have grown up this way. But I would venture to say that a majority of us have.

What is sad is that this becomes your view of God and love. If you are good and obey His Word, you feel loved. If you mess up, you feel a distance from God, and the love you enjoyed is no longer present. Your perception of love is based on the kind of love or lack thereof received from your parents.

Let me say this to you: God loves you! You cannot make God stop loving you. That is truth! In fact, when you mess up His Holy Spirit is quick to convict you about any wrong in order to keep you next to His heart in the safe place. It is not God's desire or His will that you feel unloved by Him. However, sin unchecked can cause you to feel unloved as well as ashamed. This is why God wants you to understand He loves you unconditionally.

The vision of sitting in God's lap was a proven truth of God's love for me. I was raised by hard-working parents. Dad was a farmer for the first years of my life, and then he worked away from the house for the latter years. Dad was not a man of words—I do mean none! My mother was taught and disciplined me, my older sister, and my younger brother.

Dad spoke only when we did something wrong or got in his way. I cannot recall one time when he hugged me or I sat in his lap. He was without affection toward us children as well as our mother. Dad's parents emigrated from Hungary in the early 1900s and settled in southern Louisiana as farmers. Dad was the second-born child and first-born male of nine siblings. As in many cultures, being the first-born male gave him favored status in his parents' eyes. However, having nine children did not allow for much alone or intimate time for any of the children. Even with Dad's status, he did not receive love, affection, or kind words from his parents. Their day consisted of eating, working, and survival. Sadly, Dad grew up the way he was taught. Hard work, no affection, get the job done! This demeanor carried into his life as a husband and father.

In my later years, being the middle child, I was still seeking my dad's love. Oh, I knew he loved me in his own way, but I never felt it. When I would go home to visit, there was never that knowing and assurance in my heart that I was loved by my dad. One day as I contemplated the way Dad was, God spoke to me saying, "He cannot give you what he never had." I considered what God was saying to me. As I began to see the reality and truth of God's words, I started crying. My dad never felt love. He never had affection from either of his parents. Therefore, he did not know how to love. That was a revelation of much significance to me, as I was released that day from expecting Dad to show me love. In its place, I was filled with such love for him as I realized how much he had missed. From that day forward, when I visited, I just loved my dad. I was free from expecting to be loved and was able to love in turn with no strings.

> Now to Him who is able to do exceedingly abundantly above all that we ask or think, according to the power that works in us. (Ephesians 3:20)

God loves you and me so much that He would go to the trouble of giving a woman who needed the assurance of unconditional love a vision of sitting in His lap; a vision in which He told her that He would never be angry with her; a vision that bore the fruit of love, joy, and freedom. This is how big God's love is for you as well. You are that woman. You are that man.

As for God's work being like play, if we truly trust and obey Him it is. Picture a mother and her young son of about four years of age. She takes him to the park to play on the slide, the merry-go-round, the tunnel to crawl through, and the monkey bars. As they draw near the park, his eyes light up. He immediately does what? Sits down and watches the others kids? No! He runs toward the kids and begins to join in their play. They are perfect strangers chasing one another, climbing the ladder, and sliding down over and over. You, his mother, sit near him on a bench and watch him. With a smile on your lips and in your heart, you feel his excitement. You have made your child happy, and that brings you joy.

You chat with other mothers while he is playing never taking your eyes off of your child. Then it happens. You see him trip and fall and bump heads with another child. Almost before his cry is heard, you are there, picking him up and holding him close as you whisper soothing words in his ear. You walk back to the bench, and before you can sit down he is wiggling to be set free to run and play again. He wanted your mother's compassion and the assurance, "It's going to be okay, sweetie," but no more. He wants to play. At the end of the day, when Daddy comes home, what will your son tell him? "I bumped my head today and it hurts"? I don't think so. In his excitement about the day, he will talk about how he got to play in the park. He won't remember the bumping of heads. But playing he will remember.

God said, "My work is play if you do it right." In your journey here on earth you will have bumps every day—some big, some small. You will get tired, moody, and out of sorts. God sees it all. He speaks to you, soothes you with His word, or sends a friend to be His voice. However, you do not stay there. When you speak a word to a lonely soul and see the light in their eyes, it is worth being tired. When you share a devotional and hear of a person being set free from bondage, you get excited. When a person tells you that your prayers helped to cause their loved one to get off drugs, joy floods your soul. Yes, you get tired and bump your head in life, but in the end, the fruit is worth it. You forget the bad, the time of sorrow, the pains, and your focus is centered on the joy, the love, the freedom that has come to others—all because you trusted God's love for you and obeyed Him.

I promise you that when you get to your eternal home, you won't remember one bad day. Not one! You will, however, meet many people over whom you had influence while you lived on earth, many of whom you've never met. Maybe a friend of a friend forwarded your message to them or told your story. You will hear of a word you gave to someone, a message, a smile, a hug, and how you caused them to know God in a deeper relationship or maybe for the first time. What you won't hear from anyone is how you failed, how mean you were, how you ignored them, or had no time for them. Those are the bumps on the head we all receive while on earth. God loves you. Consider that not one sparrow falls to the ground without escaping God's notice (see Matthew 10:29). Not one small bird since the beginning of time had died without His knowledge. If God loves the sparrow, His creation, that much, then consider how much more He loves you. God did not send His Son Jesus to die for a sparrow. He sent Jesus for you.

What about you?
1. Have you found yourself bound in conditional love? What will you do to change that?
2. Have you allowed past failures and whispers of failure that you will never measure up or can't get it right to keep you from drawing close to God? Can you believe God loves you in spite of your failures?
3. Will you trust God as He offers His hand to you to come and sit in His lap, trust His love for you, and allow Him to change your heart?

Make a point to stop and sit a while and soak in God. Take what I call a "soaking" CD—something slow, beautiful, and about God. Turn off the phone, the computer, and draw away with God in a quiet, undisturbed place. Do not pray. Just be there with God and let Him speak to you. In fact, there is a CD entitled *Draw Near* by Alberto and Kimberly Rivera that is an excellent soaking CD. You will find your Abba Father right there with you, eager to spend time with you, His child.

You have to live with Him day by day, and year by year, and to learn to know Him as we learn to know husbands and wives, by continual experience of a sweet and unfailing love, by many a sacred hour of interchange of affection and reception of gifts and counsels.
—Alexander MacLaren, author

CHAPTER 4

♥ LOVE NEVER FAILS

Why does God want us to know His love? If we can learn and allow this simple truth to take root in our spirit, we can learn to love rightly. If you want to "know" God, who God is, what He is like, read 1 Corinthians 13. Read it slowly and digest every word. Allow the Holy Spirit to reveal Father God to you.

I remind you how much you mean to God. "For God so loved the world [you] that He gave His only begotten Son, that whosoever [you] believes in Him, shall not perish but have everlasting life" (John 3:16). If you look closely at what love accomplishes, you see that love never fails.

> Though I speak with the tongues of men and of angels, and have not love, I am become as sounding brass, or a tinkling cymbal. (1 Corinthians 13:1)

If you sound great, speak eloquently, but love is not evident in you, God says you are nothing. You are as a loud noise with no fruit, no power—having a hollow sound. You can preach or teach the truth, but if you do so in a dogmatic (religious) manner, you have nothing, and those who have heard you received nothing of lasting value. You cannot beat the Word of God into people. However, you can sincerely love people so that they want to hear the Word.

> And though I have the gift of prophecy, and understand all mysteries, and all knowledge; and though I have all faith, so that I could remove mountains, and have not love, I am nothing. (1 Corinthians 13:3)

If you were bestowed with every gift of the Holy Spirit yet lacked love, it is counted for nothing.

> And though I bestow all my goods to feed the poor, and though I give my body to be burned, but have not love, it profits me nothing. (1 Corinthians 13:3)

If you accomplish great works, give all of your time and money, yet have no love for people, it is nothing for you or to God.

God is love! That is truth! Whether you teach, preach, instruct, counsel, pray, give of your time, or use your gifts, the first thing that must come forth is love. Love is the presence and evidence of God in you. Therefore, it is God who must be seen in you. It is love that draws people to Himself. Not your power or persuasive speech, not your giving. Not carnal, fleshly love. It is the godly love of the truth, patience, and longsuffering; it is the love in you and for you that comes through you. This is how powerful God's love is, because God is love.

This does not mean you overlook sin, but that you love the sinner with God's love, pray for them, and have compassion for them as you see their bondage to sin; as you are reminded from where you came; as you pray them out of sin. Instead of turning your back and condemning or judging them, you love them even more. Jesus came not to judge the world but to save it (see John 12:47).

God's word is truth and He cannot lie. First Corinthians 13:8 states, "Love never fails." That means God's love will not fail if you bear it within you. If this is the case (and it is because God said it), then you can see that it is Love/God who never fails. It is He who draws all men to Himself through His love in you. You are to be a vessel of love poured out to those around you so that they are drawn to His love like a magnet. Most of the time people may not understand why they are drawn to you, but they are sensing love and want to be around love. Our society today is filled with evil because of the lack of love. Those who are without God today dwell in darkness because they have no knowledge of God and His love. Why is love so important? Because our Creator God, who created man in His own image, is love.

> He who does not love does not know God, for God is love. (1 John 4:8)

> And we have known and believed the love that God has for us. God is love, and he who abides in love abides in God, and God in him. (1 John 4:16)

Cast off the works of the flesh, the pride of your gift, and seek the best gift—love. For when you are filled with Love/God then you are filled with all of Him. First Corinthians 13:13 states:

> And now abide faith, hope and love, these three; but the greatest of these is love.

Earnestly desire to love. Seek God. Seek the One who loves you so much He gave all for you while you were yet in your sin. That's love!

What about you?
1. Have you ever felt that God did not love you? How do you feel now?
2. Is love for others evident in you? If not, how will you change this?
3. How will you incorporate unconditional love into your life?

SECTION III
BORN ANEW IN CHRIST

But when "grace and truth were realized through Jesus Christ," a long-awaited revolution of the heart began to set religious captives free. Fearful bondage motivated by guilt was replaced with a fresh motivation to follow Him in truth simply out of deep devotion and delight. Rather than focusing on the accomplishments of the flesh, He spoke of the heart. Instead of demanding that the sinner fulfill a long list of requirements, He emphasized faith, if only the size of a mustard seed. The change spelled freedom, as the Lord Himself taught, "...you shall know the truth, and the truth shall make you free" (John 8:32). Rigid, barren religion was, at last, replaced by a grace-orientated, relationship-liberating grace. His followers loved it. His enemies hated it...and Him. Without a doubt, the earliest grace killers were the Pharisees.
—Charles Swindoll, The Grace Awakening

CHAPTER 5

♥ SET FREE

Dream: I was a slave in a camp where the master was harsh, mean, and instilled fear in everyone. Suddenly, as if awakening from sleep, I found myself in another place right next to the first master's camp. I knew I was in another camp and had been sold to someone else. I walked among the trees still wearing my old rags and taking in the beauty around me. I was fearful, wondering what would happen to me now. How would this new master be? A man I recognized as my old master came up to me. I was at once fearful and trembling. He said me he'd come to take me back. I was confused; I thought I was free of him. Then, another man rode up on a white horse and told the master to get out, that he had no claim or authority there. The master left angry, knowing that he had lost me.

As the rider drew closer I knew him to be the new master who purchased me from the old one. He stopped, looked down at me and smiled. He asked me if I had gone to the house to eat lunch. I replied that I had not. He looked puzzled and asked, "Why not?" I replied that I did not know I was supposed to. He then looked at me with the greatest love in his eyes and said, "Everything here is for you. You are free to partake of anything you like as you please. You are free here. Do you need anything?" In awe and trembling, I shook my head. He replied, "If you need anything, just ask for it." He smiled and rode off. I was puzzled as I contemplated his words. "Free? Ask for anything?"

Truth: "Therefore if the Son makes you free, you shall be free indeed" (John 8:36).

The white horse is a clue as to the identity of the new Master. Your Lord Jesus will come for you riding on a white horse with an army riding on white horses (see Revelation 19:11–14).

Likewise, you can be sure that the old master is Satan—the old dragon, the deceiver, the harsh taskmaster who has this world bound in sin and death (see Revelation 12:9).

The dream is a perfect picture of what happens when you are born again. You become a new creation, and you have a new Master and Lord. You are no longer in bondage living in the enemy's camp. You now live with the King of kings. You were purchased by the blood of the Son of God—Christ Jesus—redeemed from sin and death, from bondage to freedom in Christ.

> There is therefore now no condemnation to those who are in Christ Jesus, who do not walk according to the flesh, but according to the Spirit. For the law of the Spirit of life in Christ Jesus has made me free from the law of sin and death. (Romans 8:1-2)

This dream is symbolic of many people today who are saved but do not know who they are in Christ Jesus and that they are free in Him—free from sin, delivered from the bondage of fear of death and hell. Jesus became sin for you. He took your sins upon Himself, all sin committed before He was born, while He was alive, and for those who sin after His death, burial, and resurrection.

> For He made Him who knew no sin to be sin for us, that we might become the righteousness of God in Him. (2 Corinthians 5:21)

Jesus also became a curse for you. What is the curse? Read Deuteronomy 28 for the blessings and curses that follow disobedience. You will find some curses as sickness and disease, others as lack of food, children stolen from families, and on and on. Deuteronomy 28:61 states:

> Also every sickness and every plague, which is not written *[identified]* in this Book of the Law, will the Lord bring upon you until you are destroyed. (Emphasis added.)

So, we see that Jesus not only became sin for us, he also became a curse for us.

> Christ has redeemed us from the curse of the law, having become a curse for us (for it is written, "Cursed is everyone who hangs on a tree"), that the blessing of Abraham might come upon the Gentiles in Christ Jesus, that we might receive the promise of the Spirit through faith. (Galatians 3:13–14)

We cannot get any freer than the freedom Jesus has promised us.

In the previous dream I had been purchased from my old master (was saved, born again), and now I had a new Master. However, I was unaware that in my new home my new Master was good, kind, and loving. I did not know that I could eat what I wanted in His kingdom. I was told I could ask for whatever I needed in this new place. I no longer had to fear every moment of every day. In my ignorance, I expected to be treated the same as my old master treated me. This is the mind-set of many people in church today who hold religion up as a mandate of rules and regulations. They say, "Do this and you are okay with God. Mess up and you are not." When you come to the realization that there is someone who loves you, died for you, and redeemed you while you were still in sin, and that someone wants to spend time with you, then you can be free in your new home—here and now with Christ Jesus.

Too often the church preaches the salvation message, people get saved, and there it stops. Do not misunderstand. They are saved, but there is more. You must be discipled in the Word of God. I have seen young converts placed in leadership positions right away simply because they are willing to work in the church. I know of a young man who had tried many religions seeking the truth. Buddhism, Mormonism, and others. One day he went to a meeting where a man preached Jesus. As he listened, the Holy Spirit drew this young man to Christ the truth. He accepted God as the one true living God and Jesus as his Savior. Soon after his conversion, he and his wife were asked to be in charge of heading up the nursery on Sunday mornings. You might ask, What's wrong with that? What is wrong is that this man did not know the Word of God. He needed to be in Sunday school with other Christians. His grounding in faith was dependent on being taught the Word of God, not just making a profession of faith. The couple soon became discouraged and quit. They now attend church somewhere else.

As you come to the saving knowledge of Christ Jesus, you must be taught and mentored until you gain an understanding and foothold in the Word of God. In the dream, I was new in that place (a new convert). I was unaware that I was clean just because of Christ. I still saw myself as a slave in rags and in need. I was afraid to ask for anything. Why? I did not have knowledge of my new Master. I was saved, but ignorant of what that meant. Are you still a slave, in bondage to sin? The only Master you should be in bondage to now is Christ.

> And having been set free from sin, you became slaves of righteousness. (Romans 6:18)

Our Father God calls you His child—an heir to His kingdom.

> Now you are no longer a slave but God's own child. And since you are His child, God has made you His heir. (Galatians 4:7)

In one sense, you are a slave of God. I would rather think we are "love" slaves to the One who sent His Son to redeem us from the bondage of sin and death; love slaves to the One who willingly and obediently gave His life and took it up again that we might spend eternity with Him. The fruit of our love union with Christ is what He was after all along: holiness, everlasting life, in us, through Him, and for us.

> But now having been set free from sin, and having become slaves of God, you have your fruit to holiness, and the end, everlasting life. (Romans 6:22)

If you are not growing in Christ, in the Word of God, you remain saved eternally and lost at the same time. How can this be? You are saved and have eternal life, but are lost in the bondage to sin since you are ignorant of the truth of the freedom you have in Christ. You have been deceived as to who you are in Christ and do not know that that you do not have to live in bondage any longer. This is Satan's work, and he is a cruel taskmaster. If Satan cannot keep you from being saved, born again, then he will try to keep you from enjoying and walking in the fullness of your salvation. In this dream, the old master

(Satan) came back to seek that which he lost. However, the old master had to flee when confronted by truth. Indeed, once you are saved, he has no rights over you. You are God's child bought with the blood of Christ. Praise God that Jesus's blood covers us, and He has promised He will not let us go nor ever leave us.

> Let your conduct be without covetousness; be content with such things as you have. For He Himself has said, "I will never leave you nor forsake you." (Hebrews 13:5)

In Christ alone is true contentment. You can know He is always with you. You can be assured He will not leave you alone. However, your conduct should reflect your awareness of the sacrifice He made on your behalf. Only as you allow Christ to be Lord of your life can you walk in true peace and contentment. God and contentment in all situations is to be most desired.

If you know you are saved and yet feel that you're still in bondage, pray to God and ask Him to reveal His truth regarding who you are in Christ. Remember Jesus said to "ask anything." Go ahead, ask him.

> And whatever you ask in My name, that I will do, that the Father may be glorified in the Son. If you ask anything in My name, I will do it. (John 14:13-14)

You can ask in confidence knowing He hears you and will answer.

> Now this is the confidence that we have in Him, that if we ask anything according to His will, He hears us. And if we know that He hears us, whatever we ask, we know that we have the petitions that we have asked of Him. (1 John 5:14-15)

Is it God's will that you be set free from sin, death, bondage? Yes, it is. Is it God's will that you know Him and trust Him? Most certainly. Is it God's will that your family be saved from the same slavery you were once under? Absolutely! Ask Him. He's your Abba Father.

It is our Holy Father's will that you know who you are. Allow the Holy Spirit to lead you into the truth, for He is the Spirit of Truth and is given to you to know God's will and Word. In Christ you have wisdom. In Christ you are made righteous, sanctified, and redeemed. Trust Him.

> But of Him you are in Christ Jesus, who became for us wisdom from God—and righteousness and sanctification and redemption. (1 Corinthians 1:30)

Seek God for understanding. Learn His word that you may be rooted and grounded in truth. Get to know who you are in Christ Jesus that you might begin today to sing a new song, for He is worthy of your love and trust.

> And they sang a new song, saying: "You are worthy to take the scroll, and to open its seals; for You were slain, and have redeemed us to God by Your blood out of every tribe and tongue and people and nation." (Revelation 5:9)

What about you?
1. Are you walking in freedom or living in bondage? Can you see in this dream the freedom Christ offers you?
2. Do you find yourself stepping back into bondage at times? How can you overcome this?
3. Do you believe you can ask for anything in Jesus's name? What keeps you from accessing all that He has provided for you?

The supreme challenge you will face in making Christ-honoring, biblical changes is dying to self. The biblical perspective concerning "self" is exactly opposite to what the wisdom of this world proclaims.
—John C. Broger, author

CHAPTER 6

♥ DYING TO SELF

Dream: I was on the beach looking out at the ocean. I had been playing around in the water about ankle deep and then thigh deep but did not venture deeper. I did not want to get my head wet as I did not like going underwater. Yet I found myself with a strong desire to go out into the deep and swim. I wanted to let myself go, but fear of the deep kept me in the shallows. Then I overcame my fear and decided to swim out to where I could not touch bottom. I was dog-paddling trying to keep myself afloat. All of a sudden I felt hands wrap around my ankles, pulling me under the water. Shocked and terrified, I struggled to get loose and keep my head above the water, but it was no use. The hands were too strong, and I could not escape them. As I was being pulled deeper and deeper, I looked down and saw two angels pulling me down. I couldn't understand what was happening. I wanted to see the angels, but I knew I needed air. I was unable to fight against the angels as they pulled me all the way down to the bottom and held me there. I looked at them wild-eyed as I struggled to get free. I soon tired of the fight and let myself go. I saw myself let go and die, becoming totally limp, no longer having breath. Once I was dead, the angels let go of my ankles, and my body slowly rose to the top of the water. I broke through the top of the water and I was alive. I drew breath wondering what had just happened.

Truth: "I have been crucified with Christ; it is no longer I who live, but Christ lives in me; and the life which I now live in the flesh I live by faith in the Son of God, who loved me and gave Himself for me" (Galatians 2:20).

In this dream I was on the edge of the water playing and enjoying the day. However, there was a strong desire to venture into the deep. A step out in the deep with no firm ground is a step of faith. While in the shallows, I had control and stayed where it was safe. Fear of the unknown kept me from venturing deeper. I have always been a person who calculated how things worked before doing them. I observed how people did things, and then when I knew what to do I did it. I need to be in control of situations. At times, the fear of failing or being embarrassed has kept me from stepping out in faith, from allowing myself to let go and to walk in faith.

There are three types of Christians today:

First, those who simply do not desire to go deeper with God. They are content to have their salvation ensured as they sit on the sidelines watching others.

Second, there are many who want the same relationship with God that they see others have, but they are bound by fear to venture forth.

Third, there are those who desire to know God in a deeper sense, and they step out in faith in Him trusting that He will bring them into the depths of Himself. It is God who prepares your heart for this.

> Lord, You have heard the desire of the humble; You will prepare their heart. (Psalm 10:17)

In this dream, as my desire for God became stronger than my control, I ventured into the deep water (deeper things of God) where I could not touch (allowed the Spirit to move me). Yet I still had the control to keep myself above the deep. My head (mind) was determined not to give in (go under). You must give yourself (your mind, will, and emotions) totally to God in order to experience the fullness of God. It is the only way!

> For "who has known the mind of the Lord that he may instruct Him?" But we have the mind of Christ. (1 Corinthians 2:16)

There is always a struggle between your mind/flesh and the Spirit of God. It begins the day you decide to come to Christ. Satan will attempt to place many hindrances before you to confuse you as well as instill fear in you. His goal is to first keep you from taking that step toward Christ. After you obey that call of being born again in Christ Jesus, you will struggle with life events and lack of knowledge of the Word of God. The battles you experience actually rage war within your mind. It has been said that we are in a battle with Satan and the battlefield is our mind.

> But I see another law in my members, warring against the law of my mind, and bringing me into captivity to the law of sin which is in my members. O wretched man that I am! Who will deliver me from this body of death? I thank God—through Jesus Christ our Lord! So then, with the mind I myself serve the law of God, but with the flesh the law of sin. (Romans 7:23-25)

In my dream God knew that my desire to step fully into Him was greater than my controlling nature. Thus, He purposed the angels to do His will. This is for you, the body of Christ, as well. God knows your heart's desire, and when you are ready He will help you overcome the unyielding areas of your flesh. I was shocked at the angels pulling me underwater because my "old" nature was afraid of the unknown. Yet my struggling was to no avail. God's will prevailed over my fear. He will also prevail over any fear you have.

> As it is written; "Eye has not seen, nor ear heard, nor have entered into the heart of man the things which God has prepared for those who love Him." But God has revealed them to us through His Spirit. For the Spirit searches all things, yes, the deep things of God. (1 Corinthians 2:9-10)

Have you ever questioned something God was doing in your life? You didn't understand yet you knew God was in control? Sometimes you have the mind-set that you must "see" what is happening before you allow God to move in your life. This shows a lack of faith and trust in God, as well as a controlling spirit. However, out of love for you, there are times when God will reveal what He is doing, such as this dream that revealed His will for my life, as well as your life.

The angels took me to the very bottom of the ocean—as far as I could go—and held me there until I let go or yielded myself to His will. God's work will prevail in you also if you truly desire Him more than you desire yourself. Once I was dead, the angels released me to float back up to the top. It was there that I came alive. I was a new being.

When God draws you to the place where you desire to die to self, to give God your all, then He will complete the process of that death. It is a spiritual work and one that only God can accomplish. God knows everything about you. He knows when you're ready to fully surrender to Him and when you're prepared to let go as your desire for Him outweighs yourself. It is He who leads you to the ultimate death to self. He releases you into that new life in Christ. It is a life where your buoyancy is in the Holy Spirit; where you walk led by the Holy Spirit and no longer your own plans and purposes.

This is the life that God has ordained for you, but you must desire to embrace it. A life of true faith in Christ awaits you. All you have to do is step off the beach and swim out to the deep waters of faith. It is in this life that you can walk in the fulfillment of what God has called you to be in Christ, to live a life you no longer claim as your own. It is God who causes you to be equipped to walk in His fullness and fills you with the desire to obey Him.

> For it is God who works in you both to will and to do for His good pleasure. (Philippians 2:13)

You must be patient as God works in you and not let yourself be led by a spirit of impulsiveness, lest you thwart the work of God. It is His work, not yours.

> But let patience have its perfect work, that you may be perfect and complete, lacking nothing. (James 1:4)

God is working in you so that His Son will be seen in you, in every action, word, deed, and reaction. When you die to self, Jesus is revealed in you.

> For we who live are always delivered to death for Jesus' sake, that the life of Jesus also may be manifested in our mortal flesh. (2 Corinthians 4:11)

It is not only God's purpose to reveal His Son in you, it is His will for you to know the power of Christ's resurrection—to live and walk in the power of

Christ. By dying to self, you enter into the spiritual realm of knowing Him as He can be known.

> That I may know Him and the power of His resurrection, and the fellowship of His sufferings, being conformed to His death. (Philippians 3:10)

In this dream, once I stopped struggling and accepted my fate, I died. After my death I rose to the top of the water alive once again but a new creation. This is the place God wants to bring you. Trust Him. Step out in faith. Let go of self. He will resurrect you to a new life, to a living hope.

> Blessed be the God and Father of our Lord Jesus Christ, who according to His abundant mercy has begotten us again to a living hope through the resurrection of Jesus Christ from the dead. (1 Peter 1:3)

Are you content to sit on the beach and watch others venture into the deep, stepping out in faith? Or, are you ready to step into the deep and allow God to have His way with you? Dying to self may seem unattainable as you combat your flesh daily. However, God sees the desire of your heart, not the calling of your flesh. If your desire is for Him, He will bring you forth into the deep.

Smith Wigglesworth, one the great Christian preachers of our time, who walked and ministered in the miraculous, spoke on the power of Christ within, which only comes when we truly die to self. He said, "We have to be utterly slain if we want to know the resurrection power of Jesus."

What about you?

Do you desire to step out into the fullness of God? What steps will you take to do this?

1. What things have you been unwilling to let go of in order to have a deeper relationship with God?
2. What steps of faith will you take to die to self?
3. Do you understand that you can have this intimacy with God?

As the kernel of old humanity, Noah and his family, was once contained in the ark, which was tossed upon the waves of the deluge; so the kernel of the new humanity, of the new creation, Christ and His Apostles, in the little ship.
—Richard Chenevix Trench, author

CHAPTER 7

♥ A NEW CREATION

Dream: I was in a church among hundreds of people. The church seating was in itself weird. I was seated in a side section that could not see but only hear the pastor. Many others were seated there as well. I noted that most were bored and not paying attention. I remember thinking something was not right. I felt that we were not part of the service and had been put aside. When the service was over and everyone began to leave, I looked around and realized my purse was missing. I searched the area where I had been sitting and could not find it. I saw one of the deacons at the front door and walked over to him, telling him that my purse was missing. He directed me to the back of the church where there was a "Lost and Found" counter. As I walked to the back, I wondered why the church would have a lost and found counter. I spoke to the lady behind the counter saying, "My purse is missing. Someone must have picked it up. It has my ID in it as well as driver's license and credit cards." The lady said that I had to fill out some paperwork. Before she handed me the paper she wrote my name at the top of the page. As I took the paper to begin writing, I noted she wrote the name Hadashah for my name. I said, "That's not my name." She smiled and looked at me and said, "It is now."

Truth: "Therefore, if anyone is in Christ, he is a new creation; old things have passed away; behold, all things have become new" (2 Corinthians 5:17).

I woke from this dream with the name Hadashah on my mind. I thought I remembered the name as Esther's Jewish name (see Esther 2:7). In searching my concordance, I found Esther's name was Hadassah. Above it I saw Hadashah! That was the name in my dream. A slight one-letter variation in the name but totally different in meaning. In Hebrew the name given to me in the dream, Hadashah, simply means "new, fresh, new thing."

In this dream, God was revealing to me that my old identity would be taken away and a new identity and new name would now be mine. When you commit your life to Christ Jesus, you become new; you are no longer the old creation but a new creation in Christ. However, as you journey in this life on earth you grow and mature in Christ. You may go through many phases in your spiritual walk where you no longer bear the same load, the same ministry, the same workplace. As you allow yourself to be led by the Spirit, God moves you according to His will and His purposes.

> He who has an ear, let him hear what the Spirit says to the churches. To him who overcomes I will give some of the hidden manna to eat. And I will give him a white stone, and on the stone a new name written which no one knows except him who receives it. (Revelation 2:17)

The Bible speaks of many whose names were changed: Abram to Abraham (Genesis 17:5); Sarai to Sarah (Genesis 17:15); Jacob to Israel (Genesis 32:28); Daniel to Belteshazzar (Daniel 1:7); Saul to Paul (Acts 13:9); and of course, Hadassah to Esther. With each name change there was a specific change in their lives. In this dream my new name began with a change in church. I was seated in an area with people who no longer were part of that service. We were set aside. God would move us in ministry and in churches as He wills for His purposes.

My purse being stolen reflects my old identity (identification) as stolen, gone! In its place I was given a new name, Hadashah, which means exactly what was happening: "new"! In the scripture above, we see that it is the one who "overcomes" who receives a new name, new identity.

> Do not remember the former things, nor consider the things of old. Behold, I will do a new thing, now it shall spring forth; shall you not know it? I will even make a road in the wilderness and rivers in the desert. (Isaiah 43:18–19)

When God makes you a new person, He prepares the way before you. Actually, He has already prepared your way. It is just that you do not see the whole path or journey at one time. You are to go forth in Christ with a view of every day being a new day. You are not to dwell on the past, that which would keep you hobbled or stagnant in one place. You are to look to Christ as your example. Many changes occur along the way as you walk with our King Jesus.

I began life as a daughter, a newborn baby, then a child (elementary level); next a teenager, a young woman, a married woman, a mother, and a grandmother. I also became a friend, coworker, Bible teacher. You get the picture. Each phase was a different stage of my life. Each step of your life with Christ also brings something new as you grow in Him. You are to press on, as Paul reminds us, that you may be found worthy of Him.

> Not that I have already attained, or am already perfected; but I press on, that I may lay hold of that for which Christ Jesus has also laid hold of me. (Philippians 3:12)

As you press onward, along the way you are given a new name, a new path, a new direction, all in Christ. I did not stay a baby or a child with my parents. I stepped forward to embrace the next phase of my life. In Christ, you step forward knowing not everything will stay the same in your life. When you understand your life in Christ is different growth stages, you will find it easier to step forward and embrace the next phase—the new phase that is ordained for you.

You may remember Corrie ten Boom. If not, you can read this wonderful woman's story in her book *The Hiding Place*.

Corrie was a holocaust survivor. Anyone who knows her name identifies her as such. However, before she had this identification now known by the world, she was a daughter, sister, granddaughter, and friend. Then one day everything changed. It was a new day for her. It was not a good day, but it was a day for her walk with God. As we reflect on what she endured, we must look at the whole picture. Corrie survived the horror of the concentration camp while her parents and sister Betsie did not. After her release from the camp and her survival of such horror, she became a testimony of God's love and provision in Christ Jesus. She stood before hundreds of thousands of people speaking for Christ Jesus. She wrote books sharing with many the love and goodness of God. Corrie believed in God before that horrific chapter in her life. After that event, she became a new believer. Her life changed, and out of the darkness and ashes rose a woman of God who spoke of the love and grace of God as well as forgave her captors. Corrie had a new identity.

We are never left to walk new paths alone:

> His divine power has given to us all things that pertain to life and godliness, through the knowledge of Him who called us by glory and virtue. (2 Peter 1:3)

God has seen fit to equip you with everything you need to advance into the next stage of your life. Do not let fear of the unknown stop you where you are and thus, finish your life in stagnation or by living in the past. Only as you know Christ intimately can you walk into the unknown. It is He whom you trust to lead you "beside still waters and green pastures" (Psalm 23:3). Jesus is the one who walks with you through "the valley of the shadow of death" (verse 4). If you fail to trust him you become dormant in your life. You are to bring glory to God in all paths of your life.

> For you were bought at a price; therefore glorify God in your body and in your spirit, which are God's. (1 Corinthians 6:20)

You were created to bring good pleasure to God.

> For it is God who works in you both to will and to do for His good pleasure. (Philippians 2:13)

Embrace and put on the new person you are ordained to be.

> And that you put on the new man which was created according to God, in true righteousness and holiness. (Ephesians 4:24)

Do not hesitate to go forth in the new day and new phase as you are called to walk with Christ. Do not allow fear to be your partner nor stagnation your dwelling. In the gospels, we find Jesus always moving toward the next town, the next area, to preach the kingdom of God, to speak love and forgiveness to those who need to hear. Every day was a new day for Him. Every day can be a new day for you as you walk with Jesus.

Did you know that Jesus was given a new name? He was prophesied to come as "Immanuel" (God with us); as Jesus, Messiah. But in the greatest stage of His life, He is given a new name, one that only He knows.

> His eyes were like a flame of fire, and on His head were many crowns. He had a name written that no one knew except Himself. (Revelation 19:12)

He is coming again for you with His name written plainly for all to see. It is this name by which you know Him and it is He for whom you wait.

> And He has on His robe and on His thigh a name written: KING OF KINGS AND LORD OF LORDS. (Revelation 19:16)

Are you ready for a new name? Jesus knows your name.

> To him the doorkeeper opens, and the sheep hear his voice; and he calls his own sheep by name and leads them out. (John 10:3)

Will you allow Jesus to bring you to a new phase in your walk with Him? Can you let go of who you were and embrace the person Jesus wants you to be? Let go of the past, the way of life you knew, and trust Him to lead you into a new walk with Him. God will never lead you where He will not keep you. God promised this. It will be an exciting walk with never a dull moment.

What about you?
1. Are you looking to Christ as your example?
2. Have you been through a tragedy in which your life changed and you are in a new phase of your life?
3. Are you willing to allow God to make you a new person, give you a new name, and plant your feet on a new path?

*If not washed in Christ's blood and clothed in his righteousness,
no heaven for you, no heaven for me.*
—William Tiptaft, author

CHAPTER 8

♥ CLOTHED WITH CHRIST

I was in my quiet room talking to the Lord on the day of this vision. I was reading the Revelation chapter 4, where John saw a "door standing open in heaven" and then heard a voice calling, "Come up here." As I read this, I began speaking to God, saying that I wanted to come up there. Was it possible that I could come up there as John did? After a while, I got sleepy and lay back in my chair, my eyes closed with thoughts on what I had read. As I began to drift off to sleep, I was taken in a vision. I wasn't quite asleep but in a pre-sleep stage.

Vision: I was coming up through a portal or gateway into the heavens. As I rose up through the hole, I saw a hand extended to me toward my right. I looked up and knew it was Jesus. He was wearing a white robe and smiling. (As usual, there was not an identifiable face or facial features, I just knew that it was Jesus.) I placed my right hand in His left as I was rising up through this portal. I looked forward and saw at the far end of what appeared to be a walkway, a throne with someone seated on it. I knew it was God. I looked to my left and there was a line of people from where I was stood all the way to the throne of God. I recognized John the Baptist, Elijah, and Maria Woodworth-Etter (one of the first women preachers God used mightily with Holy Spirit power, preaching, and a miraculous healing ministry). I don't recall others in the line by name but recognized these three people. I was in awe, trembling, and reluctant to step forward. At this point, Maria Woodworth-Etter spoke out to encourage me, "Come on up, child!"

I stepped out into the heavens. Jesus, still holding my hand firmly, began to walk me up the pathway to the throne. Once I realized where He was taking me, I was afraid and tried to pull back. I said, "No. I'm not ready." He laughed and proceeded forward, still holding me by my hand. As we neared the throne, I was terrified and again tried to pull away, but Jesus refused to relinquish my hand. I said, "I'm not dressed," at which Jesus looked at me, smiled, and said, "Yes, you are." At this point I had two views. I was standing before God with Jesus and I was also standing on the left of God watching myself and Jesus. Then Jesus said to me, "Look!" What I saw took my breath away. I saw Jesus standing before God in a white robe. When I then looked at myself, I still saw Jesus standing there in a white robe. I saw Jesus and I saw Jesus!

Truth: "For He has clothed me with the garments of salvation, He has covered me with the robe of righteousness" (Psalm 61:10).

As a believer in Christ Jesus, you have been bathed in His cleansing blood. You now wear a white robe (the salvation and righteousness of Christ). You dwell as one in Christ, who became all for you, and His Holy Spirit lives within you. Here are a few scriptures that give you an idea of who you are in Christ.

> But of Him you are in Christ Jesus, who became for us wisdom from God—and righteousness and sanctification and redemption. (1 Corinthians 1:30)

> But you are a chosen generation, a royal priesthood, a holy nation, His own special people, that you may proclaim the praises of Him who called you out of darkness into His marvelous light. (1 Peter 2:9)

This vision was God's gracious answer to me as I desired to come up to the heavens. If you truly desire to know God and want to see God, He is more than willing to accommodate you. The question you must ask yourself is, "How great is my desire to 'know' Him?" How much of self are you willing to give up in order to enter into the holy of holies? Like in my "dying to self" dream, are you willing to go deeper, to get your head wet?

The more you let go of yourself, the more your heart's desire is to see Him and know Him, the more you will hear and see in the spirit realm. It is your Father God's heart's desire and His will that you know Him and trust Him. God wants to reveal Himself to you more than you want to see Him. Why is that? Because deep within, you know you must give up more of your own likes and dislikes, those desires of the flesh, and that is your battle today.

In this vision, Jesus was waiting for me to come up so that He might bring me forward and present me to God. He wants to present you to Abba Father today as well. As you belong to Him by faith, it is Jesus who presents you to Abba Father. It is Jesus alone who has that right.

I was given added grace to identify others who were already there. I mentioned their names in the dream. However, let me also give you their meanings: Maria Woodworth-Etter, call to Christ; John the Baptist, repentance; and Elijah, prophet and revealer of God. That I saw these three people is amazing to me. I have long read about and followed Maria Woodworth-Etter and desired to have a ministry like hers, as well as a heart for God as she had. I remind you that we shall know everyone in heaven.

> Now after six days Jesus took Peter, James, and John his brother, led them up on a high mountain by themselves; and He was transfigured before them. His face shone like the sun, and His clothes became as white as the light. And behold, Moses and Elijah appeared to them, talking with Him. (Matthew 17:1-3)

Consider the basic facts here. Moses was born and served God long before Elijah's time. Elijah was born and a prophet of God hundreds of years before Jesus's time. So, how did these two great men of God appear, not only to Jesus, but in full view of Peter, James, and John? Easy! They had heavenly bodies—bodies that would not die.

> Jesus said to her, "I am the resurrection and the life. He who believes in Me, though he may die, he shall live. And whoever lives and believes in Me *shall never die*. Do you believe this?" (John 11:25-26)

"Do you believe this?" is Jesus's question to you today. Do you really believe you shall live forever? One of the most known Bible verses is a reminder of that truth:

> For God so loved the world that He gave His only begotten Son, that whoever believes in Him should not perish but have everlasting life. (John 3:16)

Notice how Peter responds to the scene before him:

> Then Peter answered and said to Jesus, "Lord, it is good for us to be here; if You wish, let us make here three tabernacles: one for You, one for Moses, and one for Elijah." (Matthew 17:4)

Peter had not met either of these great prophets of God, and yet when Peter (in his natural flesh) saw these men, he called them by name. In other words, he recognized them. Now do you see why in the dream I was able to identify certain people? This is God's way of confirming His word to us and revealing the truth of His word. I have certainly not met the three people I saw in my vision, yet I knew who they were. This is your heavenly domain. You will know every single person there and call them by name. No strangers will be met. You are "one" in Christ.

As Jesus began to bring me forward I was in fear (reverence, yes, but also plain old fear) of God as I felt unworthy and unprepared. Do you feel unworthy at times? Not good enough? Maybe you feel as if you fail more than you are victorious? Jesus knows this. With His love, along with His beautiful smile, He would not let me go. He kept moving me forward no matter how I felt. You cannot rely on feelings when learning God's truths. Feelings will bring you back to the carnal nature quicker than any other thing. Rely on God's Word for all things. This should be a great reminder to you that it is in Christ alone that you can be ready. Your flesh, your carnal nature, will always cause you to feel unworthy of our Lord. Your great arch enemy Satan is the accuser of the brethren and delights in reminding you of your sinful ways.

When I reached the throne, I said to Jesus, "I am not dressed." I had thought that I would meet God as I am, in my fleshly and unworthy nature. But none of us meet God in our carnal nature.

> Our bodies are buried in brokenness, but they will be raised in glory. They are buried in weakness, but they will be raised in strength. (1 Corinthians 15:43)

You will have a new heavenly body.

> For in this we groan, earnestly desiring to be clothed with our habitation which is from heaven, if indeed, having been clothed, we shall not be found naked. (2 Corinthians 5:2–3)

It is God who prepares you for your wedding day with Christ, and you can have confidence that you will be with Him.

> Now He who has prepared us for this very thing is God, who also has given us the Spirit as a guarantee. So we are always confident, knowing that while we are at home in the body we are absent from the Lord. For we walk by faith, not by sight. (2 Corinthians 5:5–7)

You can be confident that as you stand before God He will only see Jesus. He will see that His Son covered your sins and paid the price for you. You will be clothed with the righteousness of Christ—His righteousness. Look back at the dream and see your master pattern. Christ has drawn you to Himself, and you receive Him into yourself. You "put on" Christ.

> For you are all sons of God through faith in Christ Jesus. For as many of you as were baptized into Christ have put on Christ. (Galatians 3:26–27)

As you abide "in Christ" you are a new creation.
> Therefore, if anyone is in Christ, he is a new creation; old things have passed away; behold, all things have become new. (2 Corinthians 5:17)

You are seated with Christ now spiritually.

> [God] raised us up together, and made us sit together in the heavenly places in Christ Jesus. (Ephesians 2:6)

Paul states "made you" not "going to make you." This is a now word! In the Spirit you can access heaven now, today. You can "go up" if you truly believe and desire to do so in your heart. When Abba Father looks on you (right now), He sees His Son Jesus.

> Beloved, now we are children of God; and it has not yet been revealed what we shall be, but we know that when He is revealed, we shall be like Him, for we shall see Him as He is. (1 John 3:2)

You will be dressed in a white robe signifying purity, holiness, and righteousness before God as you are covered by the blood of Christ.

> After these things I looked, and behold, a great multitude which no one could number, of all nations, tribes, peoples, and tongues, standing before the throne and before the Lamb, clothed with white robes, with palm branches in their hands. . . . Then one of the elders answered, saying to me, "Who are these arrayed in white robes, and where did they come from?" And I said to him, "Sir, you know." So he said to me, "These are the ones who come out of the great tribulation, and washed their robes and made them white in the blood of the Lamb." (Revelation 7:9–14)

There is no other way that you can be made pure, holy, and blameless except through Christ's blood atonement. By your personal acceptance, by faith, of what Christ did on that cross for you can His blood make you white as snow. Do you deserve this? No. No one does. Christ is God's love gift to and for you. This gift can only be received by faith. The Word says in Galatians 3:27: "For as many of you as were baptized into Christ have put on Christ."

When God looks at you He sees Jesus.

What about you?
1. Are you willing to allow Christ to bring you into a heavenly vision?
2. Do you understand you are clothed in the righteousness of Christ?
3. Do you feel you look like Jesus to God? What hinders you from believing this?

SECTION IV
CHRIST'S EXAMPLE

*Christ is the key which unlocks the golden doors into
the temple of Divine truth.*
—*A. W. Pink, author*

CHAPTER 9

♥ THE OPEN DOOR

It was the eve of Yom Kippur 2004. My friend Sherry and I had taken the weekend to draw away to hear the Lord speak to us concerning Yom Kippur, the upcoming Jewish New Year. Also called the Day of Atonement, Yom Kippur is the holiest day of the year for Jews and concludes the annual High Holy Days, a period of repentance, prayer, and fasting.

Here we were at six p.m., the beginning of Yom Kippur, at the edge of a lake to take communion together. We stood there for a while just listening with expectation for God to speak to us. I seated myself on the ground while Sherry stood and looked out over the water. After a few minutes, Sherry said, "He's here. Do you smell that?" I looked up at her wondering what she smelled when a fragrance passed by me. It was one that had not been present before. It was the sweetest fragrance. I was awed and humbled knowing our Lord Jesus was with us.

After communion, we spent the next few hours on the back deck talking, singing, writing, allowing the Lord to speak to us. We separated and went to our bedrooms. I lay down in my bed and began to pray. I dozed off around eleven p.m. I woke up suddenly and realized I had been dreaming. I looked at the clock and I had only been asleep for about ten minutes. I do not know if this was a dream, a vision, or a real life experience, so I will refer to it as a dream.

Dream: I was in bed right where I was at that moment in time. I saw the bedroom door was opened partially and Jesus stood there. He was in a white robe that came to His feet and His hair was semi-long, below His ears but not to His shoulders. Though His facial features were not identifiable, I knew it was Jesus. In His right hand He held a gold chalice, while at the same time His hand was in an open slot (instead of door knob) in the door. He spoke. "See. With this cup I can open this door."

Truth: "Therefore, brethren, having boldness to enter the Holiest by the blood of Jesus, by a new and living way which He consecrated for us, through the veil, that is, His flesh, and [having] a High Priest over the house of God, let us draw near with a true heart in full assurance of faith, having our hearts sprinkled from an evil conscience and our bodies washed with pure water" (Hebrews 10:19-22).

I awoke with a start, realizing I had dozed off and had this dream or encounter. The Lord Jesus had just been there. This was a "now" dream happening right where I was, in the room I was in, and in "now" time. My immediate thought was, "Jesus was in my room. Right here, right now." I lay there contemplating what Jesus said. I knew that this was not just a dream of symbolism but that Jesus was giving me a message: "See? With this cup I can open this door."

I did not understand this dream for some years. I have thought on it, prayed about it, and forgot it, then remembered it and let it go again. Until this book.

In the Word of God we find Jesus praying to His Father God three times about a cup passing from Him. All of this took place in the Garden of Gethsemane on the eve of His crucifixion.

> He went a little farther and fell on His face, and prayed, saying, "O My Father, if it is possible, let this cup pass from Me; nevertheless, not as I will, but as You will." . . . Again, a second time, He went away and prayed, saying, "O My Father, if this cup cannot pass away from Me unless I drink it, Your will be done." (Matthew 26:39-42)

We find the same words in Mark 14:36 and Luke 22:42.

Jesus's cup of suffering was the cross, embraced when He knew death was inevitable. Some think that Jesus was unaware of what He was going to go through. Scripture tells us He was fully aware and even discussed it with Moses and Elijah.

> And behold, two men talked with Him, who were Moses and Elijah, who appeared in glory and spoke of His decease which He was about to accomplish at Jerusalem. (Luke 9:30-31)

Jesus was not anxious to embrace death. He was human. At the point of his praying, He was the "son of man." His pain and suffering is not something any human being would choose, especially the kind of torture He knew He was going to go through. However, Jesus's last words in these verses were always at the forefront of all that He did. "Nevertheless, not my will but your will be done," He spoke to His Father.

"With this cup I can open this door." What door did Jesus open? Because of Jesus's death, burial, resurrection, and ascension, the door to your Abba Father has been opened. While He hung on the cross, the temple veil was torn in two from top to bottom. This tearing of the veil allows you to enter into the Holy of Holies, to Abba Father, once and for all. Because sin was laid upon Christ Jesus and He became sin as well as the curse for us (see Galatians 3:13), the door is open for you to believe in Him and enter into the kingdom of God for eternity. For you, the door is Jesus. In John 10:9, he tells us:

> I am the door. If anyone enters by Me, he will be saved, and will go in and out and find pasture.

Jesus desired God's will more than His own. He took the cup He was given, and by drinking and embracing it, He was able to open the door, the way, for all mankind, all nations, to enter into communion with Himself, with Father God. Jesus provided the way and the freedom to walk in the truth.

What about your door? What doors have you shut and think Jesus does not know about, cannot see? There is nothing hidden from God.

> And there is no creature hidden from His sight, but all things are naked and open to the eyes of Him to whom we must give account. (Hebrews 4:13)

Because of Jesus's obedience to Father God, His acceptance of the cup in His life, He is able to walk through any door of your life. Afraid of what man may think, how many times have you allowed issues, acts, and your past to remain hidden in the closet of your soul? Maybe for emotional reasons, you do not want to deal with those hidden places. These doors may seem to be solidly shut within, but they are strongholds that keep you in bondage. They keep you from moving onto higher ground in your walk with Jesus. All of these hidden things have been paid for by Jesus at the cross. In reality, they are skeletons, dead issues. They have no life nor part in your life any longer. Jesus knocks on the door of your heart and asks to come in.

You may have seen the painting of Jesus knocking at the door. In that picture, there is no door handle on the outside. The door is your heart. He knocks, and you must respond by opening the door and inviting Him in.

First, Jesus knocks on your heart's door when you are an unbeliever so that you may know Him and have eternal life with Him. After salvation, He knocks on your heart because of issues that you have not allowed to come to light, the things you don't want to give up. He wants to release you from all that keeps you from being free in the Son of God (John 8:36, 38). Jesus is your freedom. He is the "way, the truth, and the life and no one comes to the Father except through [Him]" (John 14:6).

Jesus opened the door to freedom from sin's rule and reign in your life. You do not have to walk in that realm anymore. Your pathway of life before knowing Christ has many stones in the road and closed closets that you dare not reveal. If you try to drag these hindrances along into your new life with Christ, you find your freedom appears fleeting. Why is this? The hidden, unconfessed sins compete with Christ as master of your life.

Webster's dictionary defines the word freedom as "exemption from a specified obligation or discomfort." The cup Jesus embraced and the door He opened to you is complete and absolute freedom in Christ Jesus. You are exempt from paying the obligatory sin debt of death and hell and the obvious horror of it, a horror that man cannot begin to imagine. Make no mistake—there is a hell and it is a living, eternal suffering. The price for your life was the blood of Christ—every single drop.

> For you were bought at a price; therefore glorify God in your body and in your spirit, which are God's. (1 Corinthians 6:20)

You were bought at a price; do not become slaves of men. (7:23)

Until you comprehend the love that Abba Father has for you, the price He paid for you, you will continue to keep some doors in your life shut. Your fear will not allow Christ to touch on those closed areas, much less open them. Fear is a strong master. Only as you trust Christ with your whole being can you experience the cleansing and freedom you desire.

> Then Jesus said to those Jews who believed Him, "If you abide in My word, you are My disciples indeed. And you shall know the truth, and the truth shall make you free." (John 8:31-32)

As you take this step of faith allowing Jesus to open the door to your heart and soul, to purify you, you will bear fruit unto holiness.

> But now having been set free from sin, and having become slaves of God, you have your fruit to holiness, and the end, everlasting life. (Romans 6:22)

There is no true freedom unless Christ Jesus is at the helm of your life. By drinking of the cup given to Him, Jesus embraced His crucifixion, burial, and resurrection. This is the cup by which He has opened the door for you to enter behind the veil to Abba Father. This door allows you to enter into communion and fellowship with our Holy Sovereign God. Today, would you invite Jesus further entrance into your life that those old, musty smelling closets of your life, the memories of bondage, of fear, of past mistakes, may be cleaned out forever?

If you open the door to your heart, you will find Jesus opening doors for you.

What about you?
1. Are you trusting Jesus with all of your life, or are you holding something back?
2. Has fear kept some doors in your life sealed and closed? Will you give Jesus the authority to open them and deal with them?
3. What hindrances keep you from being truthful with Jesus?

I wish, brothers and sisters, that we could all imitate "the pearl oyster"—A hurtful particle intrudes itself into its shell, and this vexes and grieves it. It cannot reject the evil, but what does it do but "cover" it with a precious substance extracted out of its own life, by which it turns the intruder into a pearl! Oh, that we could do so with the provocations we receive from our fellow Christians, so that pearls of patience, gentleness, and forgiveness might be bred within us by that which otherwise would have harmed us.
—Charles Spurgeon, author

CHAPTER 10

♥ LOVE YOUR BRETHREN

Dream: I was seated in an enclosed arena where events such as horse shows and barrel riding take place. I was seated on the side of the arena in the end seat on the third row. I sat in excitement as I knew Jesus was coming there that day. As I waited, I looked around and saw that there were very few people present. I wondered why the arena was not packed. Didn't the people know Jesus was going to be there today? The people who were present were laughing and cutting up. I heard some rough talking and felt disappointed. I looked to my right and saw Jesus as He walked into the arena on the ground level. He was wearing a long white tunic that came to His feet and had mid-shoulder length hair. He looked up and our eyes met. I kept my eyes on Him as He started up the steps. He stopped beside my seat. I looked up at Him, and He smiled at me. I looked into His eyes, and the love that I saw was so overwhelming that I could not speak. He just smiled at me allowing His eyes to speak to me. After about five seconds, He moved upward toward the top of the seating area. I sat there lost in the love that I had just seen. Love—for me! My thoughts were interrupted as I heard laughing. I turned and looked upward behind me. Jesus was sitting behind two people who were laughing and having a good time. To my mind, they did not seem to understand who Jesus was. As my eyes met His, though it was not spoken, I knew in my spirit He was saying, "See. I love them too."

Truth: "But you shall love your neighbor as yourself" (Leviticus 19:18). "But I say to you, love your enemies, bless those who curse you, do good to those who hate you, and pray for those who spitefully use you and persecute you" (Matthew 5:44).

Do you tend to judge others by their actions? Admit it. You know you have. Maybe you judged that lady's hair, someone's dress code, that man's integrity, the way someone spoke. You even judge your spouse on what they do or how they do things. You are not alone. We all do it, and we all are wrong. Jesus commanded us not to judge but to love. Somehow Christians have even gotten this one backward. We mostly judge and rarely love.

> Judge not, that you be not judged for with what judgment you judge, you will be judged; and with the measure you use, it will be measured back to you. (Matthew 7:1-2)

If you receive the Bible as God's Word, you will think twice before you judge someone else—regardless of whether that person is right or wrong. In this dream Jesus's lesson was to help you and me understand that He loves everyone. Just because someone hasn't come to know Jesus yet, or maybe not as well as you, does not mean He doesn't love them. Jesus gave this revelation as an example of how to love our fellow man, our brethren. You should always be mindful that God's love, His gift of His Son, and the Holy Spirit draws men to Jesus.

Pride can cause you to make the mistake of believing Jesus loves only those who have made a commitment to Him. This is not so. Jesus loves all mankind. It is just that all don't know this or understand and have yet to come to Him. It is your job as a Christian to "love them" to Jesus and not judge them to hell.

Look within and consider how your love compares to Jesus's command. Do you feel you need to renovate your love? Maybe you might be missing a few parts? It is safe to say that your carnal love will never measure up to God's love. This is why God desires you to "abide in Christ and He in you" (John 15:5). Without the vital connection of abiding, you can do nothing. Why? Because it is love (God is love) that never fails (1 Corinthians 13:8). When you abide in Christ and He in you, then God's love through Christ flows into you as well as from you. Sounds simple, doesn't it? When you run your life, you can be sure that doubt, anger, judging, and more will be present and become the star players in your actions. When you abide in Christ and His love, then peace, joy, and love are present in your life. This is the fruit of abiding in Christ.

God's love is total—all encompassing. Too often you might look for love through feelings. God's love is always there. It never leaves. So what is the problem? The key to many problems in this world has to do with your physical senses. Have you ever said, "I don't feel loved" or "I feel they are mad at me"? I think most people have at one time or another. God tells His children repeatedly to "walk by faith not by sight" (2 Corinthians 5:7). Your flesh desires to see and feel everything just as the Greeks in the biblical times did. They resisted faith and had to have hands-on, touchy-feely things. Thus, even their type of worship was sensual, feeling, worship of self, and eventually became perverted and totally self-focused, self-worship.

Besides God's vast love for you, He also wants you to know that you can come to him and ask anything in Jesus's name. Note below that Jesus reiterated "anything."

> And whatever you ask in My name, that I will do, that the Father may be glorified in the Son. If you ask anything in My name, I will do it. (John 14:13–14)

You must ask in faith believing God, believing Jesus, and ask in His name and according to His will.

> Now this is the confidence that we have in Him, that if we ask anything according to His will, He hears us. And if we know that He hears us, whatever we ask, we know that we have the petitions that we have asked of Him. (1 John 5:14–15)

> Faith is the substance of things hoped for (believing) the evidence of things not seen. (Hebrews 11:1)

Our faith should say, "God said it and I believe it." Faith in God often falters, not only because you want to "see" something, feel something, but worse, you want to know what God is going to do before you accept His will. At God's *promise*, Abraham stepped out in faith leaving his own people to travel to a *promised* land to have a *promised* son and *promised* seeds to come. He did not know where he was going or how long it would take to get there. He only knew God promised, and he chose to believe God.

Every promise you need is right before you. However, you must step out in faith. Do you tend to refuse to step out in faith and instead wait for a "sign"? Maybe you beg and plead with God to show you something even though He has already spoken. Doubt is a killer. It will kill God's promises to you and your faith in God. James has a lot to say about asking of God and doubting God at the same time.

> But let him ask in faith, with no doubting, for he who doubts is like a wave of the sea driven and tossed by the wind. For let not that man suppose that he will receive anything from the Lord; he is a double-minded man, unstable in all his ways. (James 1:6–8)

God's word is all life and all power. (Hebrews 4:12). You must learn to hear His voice, discern the way, and step out as led by the Holy Spirit. When doubt comes, and it surely will as long as Satan is free on this earth, you must see it for what it is—a lie from hell. It is only as Jesus abides in you and you in Him, in love, that you can stand firm in faith. In Ephesians 3:17–19, Paul prays:

> That Christ may dwell in your hearts through faith; that you, being rooted and grounded in love, may be able to comprehend with all the saints what is the width and length and depth and height—to know the love of Christ which passes knowledge, that you may be filled with all the fullness of God.

Knowing Christ's love goes far beyond knowledge (learned things) and is first received by faith. When you look at the very act of the cross embraced by our Lord Jesus, you cannot deny the love He has for you, not only then but now. Your faith received this act by Christ as real and accomplished for you. You were not present at the crucifixion nor did you feel the excruciating pain Jesus endured. Yet, by faith you believe in what Christ did for you and enjoy eternal life today. This is the greatest faith one can have. Believing in an act that was completed more than two thousand years ago, something you did not see but by faith receive as truth, gives you eternal life with God.

I have heard people say they did not have much faith or their faith was weak. How is your faith? If you consider the faith you have to believe Jesus is the Messiah, you are abundantly rich in faith. You have a lot of faith! Receiving this revelation of faith, you can go forward with the same power of faith in your daily life. Your faith is not weak. You believe in Christ Jesus as your Savior, therefore your faith is whole. When you say you have no faith or weak faith, you have believed a lie. Your faith and hope are in God through faith in Jesus.

> He indeed was foreordained before the foundation of the world, but was manifest in these last times for you who through Him believe in God, who raised Him from the dead and gave Him glory, so that your faith and hope are in God. (1 Peter 1:20-21)

If you allow faith to rule in your heart instead of feelings (what you see or touch), then follows the promise "that you may be filled with all the fullness of God" (Ephesians 3:19). As you allow the love of Christ to dwell deeply and fully within you, by faith, you can know God's fullness, which is expressed only in and through Christ Jesus.

> For in Him dwells all the fullness of the Godhead bodily; and you are complete in him, who is the head of all principality and power. (Colossians 2:9-10)

Wow! Think about that. In your union with Christ, through His empowering Spirit, you are complete. Not going to be—are! Now! You have all the fullness of God available to you, but you must appropriate that fullness through faith. Paul's prayer for the Ephesians is also for you today. You can ask the Holy Spirit to fill every aspect of your life to the fullest today.

Paul says God's love is total and is found in Christ. You should desire this love to permeate every corner of your life. It is high, it is deep, it is wide, and it is long. In other words, there is no place you can go and not have the love of Christ, as it is endless. A footnote in the New King James Life Application Study Bible expresses Christ's love this way:

- Its width covers the breadth of our own experience, and it reaches to the whole world.
- Its length continues the length of our lives.
- Its depth reaches to the depths of discouragement, despair, and even death.
- Its height rises to the heights of our celebration and elation.

It is God's will and His heart's desire that you know Him. Why? Because if you know God, you know love. Again, "He who does not love does not know God, for God is love" (John 4:8, 16).

Trust His Word. Act on His Word by faith. Allow His Holy Spirit to lead. As you abide in His love, your heart will open, not only to your brethren but to your enemies as well. To not love your enemies is disobedience and an unfruitful life.

> But if you love those who love you, what credit is that to you? For even sinners love those who love them. (Luke 6:32)

In learning to abide in love, you will be able to obey the command to judge not.

> Judge not, and you shall not be judged. Condemn not, and you shall not be condemned. Forgive, and you will be forgiven. (Luke 6:37)

In the dream I understood that Jesus loves all mankind. He wanted me to understand this and follow His example—even to praying for my enemies and doing good to them.

> But I say to you, love your enemies, bless those who curse you, do good to those who hate you, and pray for those who spitefully use you and persecute you. (Matthew 5:44)

Loving your brethren, saved and unsaved, is a direct act of obedience that bears the fruit of giving glory unto our Lord Jesus.

What about you?
1. Is there someone in your life you have been unable to love? How will you rectify that situation?
2. Have you experienced Jesus's love? Did you share it with others?
3. Have you thought about what the crucifixion was like for Jesus? Do you understand why He did this?

To be a Christian is not only to believe the teaching of Christ, and to practice it; it is not only to try to follow the pattern and example of Christ; it is to be so vitally related to Christ that His life and His power are working in us. It is to be "in Christ," it is for Christ to be in us.
—Martyn Lloyd-Jones, author

CHAPTER 11
♥ JESUS IS OUR EXAMPLE

Dream: I was at a Bible conference that had just ended. As I walked to my car, I said to my friend Sherry Henderson, "I'm not sure of the way home so I'm going to follow you." She replied, "Okay. I'm following Joe." (Joe Medina is a prophet and Bible teacher whose studies I attended for three years and where the Word of God came alive in my spirit. It is where I learned about the prophetic realm, dreams, and visions. God had placed me for a season where I needed to be.)

The three of us were in our own cars. I got into my car prepared to follow Sherry. However, because of everyone leaving at the same time, I was unable to pull out into traffic to get directly behind her. Once I was able to get onto the main road, I could see Joe's vehicle a short way ahead and Sherry's behind him. A car pulled out in front of me causing me to come to a stop. I tried to see where Joe and Sherry were, but they were no longer in my vision.

As I was stopped, a man opened my passenger door, got in, and said, "I'll show you the way home." I wondered how he knew I needed help. I began to drive when he said, "Make a right here." I said, "Joe and Sherry did not turn here." He replied, "I know, but I have to make a stop. I'll get you home." I turned right, and he directed me to stop in front of a house. He got out of the car, opened its trunk, and removed a basket of fruit and vegetables. I glanced back toward my trunk and wondered where the food came from. I knew it was not in my trunk before.

He proceeded to the door of the house and knocked. A lady came to the door he gave her the basket of food. I could see she was thrilled and kept thanking him over and over. The man got back into my car and directed me to drive on until we came to another house further down. We again came to a stop where he retrieved another basket of vegetables from the trunk and took it to the front door.

When he was back in the car, I asked him what he was doing. He replied, "Meeting these people's needs." We traveled on like this giving out food to certain houses that had a need. I was puzzled as he seemed to know exactly which homes were needy.

Truth: "Then the master said to the servant, 'Go out into the highways and hedges, and compel them to come in, that my house may be filled'" (Luke 14:23).

You are never to follow a person or a ministry. You are to follow Jesus. How many times have you gotten caught up in someone else's way of doing things, imitating their pattern and ways, maybe followed someone who is in ministry, traveling from church to church, or even state to state to hear them? Sometimes this can be good; you can learn by hearing others and by fellowship with like minds in Christ. However, when you do not learn to eat on your own and continually live your spiritual life dependant on what some other person says or does, you are skating on thin ice, so to speak. In other words, if you do not learn what God wants from you and for you, then you will emulate man and not Christ.

> All Scripture is given by inspiration of God, and is profitable for doctrine, for reproof, for correction, for instruction in righteousness, that the man of God may be complete, thoroughly equipped for every good work. (1 Timothy 3:16–17)

In this dream I was attempting to follow Sherry and Joe. Both of these two people played a major part in my spiritual growth. Your growth in Christ is similar in how you learned to physically walk. At first, you need hands-on help to hold you. You learn how to stand, but only with help. You begin to take steps, but fall frequently. Hands are there to help you up. Then comes the day when your legs are sturdy and strong and your stance is stable. You are able to walk without help. When you are first saved, God will place people in your life to teach and mentor you in your spiritually walk. They will answer questions and point you to truth as you learn how to hear God and how to be led by the Holy Spirit. When God knows you are ready, you will begin to walk your own path as ordained by God. You were given a foundation in Christ by helpers until such time as you could walk on your own. Now you are able to go forward in your own spiritual strength and not rely upon a person for help. This does not mean you will never need to confer with someone, but it does mean you are now able to help others come to the place that you have reached.

Note that Joe, Sherry, and I each had our own car. In prophetic messages today, many times a car is symbolic of your personal ministry. This is the case in this dream. We were together at the conference but separate in our vehicles/ministry, in God's plans for us individually. God purposefully hindered me from following others. The familiar is hard to let go of, but it must be loosed so that God can bring you to the next phase in your walk with Him. He wanted me to learn to walk on my own with His leading, just as He desires you to learn to follow Him.

The man leading me was Jesus or perhaps the Holy Spirit. Although I was unaware of who He was when He got into my car, I trusted him. He led me off the road traveled by others and onto unfamiliar highways and byways. Trusting the Holy Spirit's leading is the only way you can be sure the path you are on is the correct one.

One of the hardest things for many is believing that God will lead them, or even believing they are hearing correctly, especially when they see others they admire doing something different. You might question yourself because no one seems to see what you see or hear what you see and hear. This does not make you wrong. Sometimes you can get caught up in another person's boldness and flamboyant personality and think they must know better than you. You must trust God with your life in order to walk the path He has for you. There have been many times when I saw things in a different light than my peers, but I gave in to their leading only to find later that what I had seen or heard was correct to begin with. This is a way of learning to trust God for yourself.

The man took food out of my trunk that I was not conscious of having. This represents fruit that is built up and stored within you that you are not using. Every time you help someone know God, you are bearing fruit to Jesus. In retrieving this food from the trunk, He was reaching within me for fruit that was stored there. When God deems you ready to walk on your own, Jesus will pull forth the fruit within you to assist others in their walk. His giving of food to the needy is an example of what you are to be doing in His name. As the food was in my car, He was revealing to me that I had something to give. You might feel inadequate to speak, teach, or help others, but you are not. You are filled with the Holy Spirit of God. The Spirit teaches and leads you to accomplish that which you are called to do. Within you is provision, not only for your own life, but for those around you. As you abide in Christ, that provision multiplies. This is the heart of Christ and the reality of ministry. You see the need of someone else and you give out of yourself to help them.

Ask yourself this question: "Am I doing what God called me to do?" You are called, equipped, and gifted by God for His purposes and for His glory, and it is God who will complete the work in you.

> [Be] confident of this very thing, that He who has begun a good work in you will complete it until the day of Jesus Christ. (Philippians 1:6)

If you know you are not walking in your calling, or don't understand what your calling is, you need to spend some intimate time with God and find what it is He has gifted you to do.

> I, the Lord, have called you in righteousness, and will hold your hand; I will keep you and give you as a covenant to the people, as a light to the Gentiles. (Isaiah 42:6)

Jesus is the true Light for all mankind. When you are saved, you bear the light of Christ within you.

> For you were once darkness, but now you are light in the Lord. Walk as children of light. (Ephesians 5:8)

Jesus says "follow me" nineteen times in the New Testament. Note that this is a command not a suggestion. If your desire is to accomplish God's will and purpose, to find your contentment in the ministry you are given, you must follow His lead. When you determine to obey this command, Jesus will lead you in ways you never dreamed—through valleys and over mountains with breathtaking views as you keep your eyes on Him. Jesus has an exciting plan for your life. Will you step out and follow Him?

What about you?
1. Is there someone in your life you follow instead of Jesus?
2. Are you willing to trust Jesus to lead you where He wants you to go?
3. What provisions do you have (talents, gifts) that you are not using? Will you allow Jesus to use them for the brethren?

It is in the deepest darkness of the starless midnight that men learn how to hold on to the hidden Hand most tightly and how that Hand holds them; that He sees where we do not, and knows the way He takes; and though the way be to us a roundabout way, it is the right way.
—A. T. Pierson, author

CHAPTER 12

♥ ALL THAT GLITTERS IS NOT GOLD

Dream: I was walking hand in hand with Jesus. He was on my right. I was about twelve years of age. As we walked, I looked ahead and saw in the distance something that appeared to be huge with lights flashing, objects glittering, and multiple colors, much like a carnival setting. I was immediately captivated by it and with excitement began to walk faster. However, I noticed that Jesus did not move with me as I purposed to hurry, nor did He let go of my hand.

I looked up at Him, and He smiled at me. I was puzzled thinking, "Don't you see that?" Once again, I tried to pull him toward the object of my desire. Instead, He began to walk off the path to the right. Again, He would not let go of my hand. We walked to the right going forward in the direction of our course, and I could see we were going to go around the object. I was disappointed as I did not understand why Jesus did not want to go see the beautiful, bright object. We continued to walk as I longingly looked to my left at the brightly lit object. (I was like a child who passes a carnival with parents who would not stop. I'm sure you've all been there. You've also been the parent who kept going while your children stared at the carnival with bated breath, hoping you would stop but disappointed and not understanding why you didn't.)

By this time, with great reluctance, I allowed Jesus to pull me along with Him. As we began to pass beyond the front of the object, I gasped in horror as I saw the back of it. It was black, ugly, and had a sinister appearance. I knew it was not a place I wanted to be. With my hand firmly held by Jesus, we continued to walk, and I was amazed that the object I thought was so beautiful was actually a menacing deception.

Truth: "The kingdom of God is not eating and drinking, but righteousness and peace and joy in the Holy Spirit" (Romans 14:17).

"All that glitters is not gold" is a phrase you have heard or said to someone else, and it is a true statement. You might see a beautiful gold ring and be captured by its beauty, only to find out it is a dime-store toy with no value and no depth. How many times are women attracted by a glittering diamond ring, bracelet, or earrings? Jewels of all kinds fascinate the eye and the heart of many. How often is a man captivated by a woman's outside appearance only to find the inside so shallow he was sorry once he embraced her? There are several things about this dream that stand out. One, I was a child. Jesus says, "Come as a child." It is with a true child's heart that we trust Jesus completely and follow Him.

I was with my husband and his family one night at a restaurant. As we ate and talked, I noted a family about ten feet from us getting ready to leave. The father was standing up holding his baby, who appeared to be around seven months old. He was holding his child against his side with the baby hanging over his arm staring around the room with complete contentment. I was caught up in the visual of this man and his child. As I watched the father and his baby, I thought, "This is how we should be with our Father God. We are to trust Him completely, knowing He will keep a firm grip on us, never drop us or let us go, no matter what our circumstances." I watched in fascination as the baby cooed and giggled, pumping its legs and waving its arms all the while having no fear or even knowledge of danger.

In the dream above, Jesus refused to let go of my hand. No matter how much I pulled, He would not let me go. Is this not an awesome picture of our Lord? I was captivated by the glittering lights, the flashing colors, and the initial appearance of what I saw. With no more thought, I immediately decided we needed to go there. Jesus had other plans and refused to let go of my hand. Disappointed as any child is when they don't get what they want, I succumbed to His lead. I did not understand why Jesus could not see how much fun this would be. Little did I know His vision was very clear. He saw the deception, the temptation, and the evil that appeared good, fun, and acceptable but was in fact bad, deadly, and wrong. It was a false hope designed to blow me off course. That which appeals to your eye and captures your attention can so easily be a snare. Had I been allowed to follow my own nature without thinking, I would have been trapped in a situation or place that was not God's will for me.

> For he is cast into a net by his own feet, and he walks into a snare. (Job 18:8)

There are times when our Lord will prevent you from reaching a destination or keep you from gravitating to a situation that He knows is not good. He will keep a firm hold on your hand and on your heart by leading you through the power of His Holy Spirit. That is not to say you will never run off and do something you shouldn't. However, if you are in tune to the Spirit's leading, it will be harder for you to pull away. I could have jerked my hand away or pulled harder, but I knew He did not want me to go that way. As disappointed as I was and though I questioned Him, I followed His lead looking unto Him.

> Therefore we also, since we are surrounded by so great a cloud of witnesses, let us lay aside every weight, and the sin which so easily ensnares us, and let us run with endurance the race that is set before us, looking unto Jesus, the author and finisher of our faith, who for the joy that was set before Him endured the cross, despising the shame, and has sat down at the right hand of the throne of God. (Hebrews 12:1-2)

If you learn to trust Jesus in this way, your resistance to temptation will be stronger. However, there is much to learn in the way of obedience, is there not? Your first lesson should be to learn that temptations will come and where they come from.

> Let no one say when he is tempted, "I am tempted by God"; for God cannot be tempted by evil, nor does He Himself tempt anyone. But each one is tempted when he is drawn away by his own desires and enticed. Then, when desire has conceived, it gives birth to sin; and sin, when it is full-grown, brings forth death. Do not be deceived, my beloved brethren. (James 1:13-16)

Many of the things that we tend to think are good are not. Sin looks good, inviting, and is even pleasurable—for the moment. After sin's consummation it becomes ugly, vile, and affects your mind and emotions. Too late, you wish you had not succumbed to it.

Many a person has entered into sexual immorality only to find the after effects are not worth it. The lying, cheating, and stealing away from a spouse leads to anxiety and guilt. Sadly, families are torn apart because of the enticing and deadly call of immoral living. Oh, it looks good. "That man, that woman, is so nice. They understand me. I've never felt this way before." The longer you entertain eating of the proverbial forbidden fruit, the deeper the hooks of temptation sink in and pull you to step across the boundary of the trap until it is too late. The results are deadly to a marriage, to the values of the children, and even at times carry uninvited diseases with it. One desire. One act. Much is ruined.

Because of its strong allure, think how often you have chosen sin only to find that in place of pleasure a root of bitterness and self-loathing took root. This is what the dream reveals. The object looked good, bright, fun, something that caught my eye as well as my heart. However, underneath its shallow concealment was death, ugliness, vileness, and all that is not of God. This is not the path Jesus chooses for you and well you know it. You know what sin is. However, like the object in my dream, sin still beckons at times, trying to gain a foothold in your life. You must walk with wisdom. The word *wisdom* is found 227 times in the Bible.

> How much better to get wisdom than gold! And to get understanding is to be chosen rather than silver. (Proverbs 16:16)

Even though I was only a twelve-year-old child in the dream, I had wisdom. Did I use wisdom in the dream? Yes, I did. You might ask, how? In not pulling my hand out of Jesus's hand, wisdom prevailed. Though I was disappointed, I knew that no matter what, Jesus knew best. As we abide in Jesus, we abide in wisdom. Jesus is the wisdom of God.

> But to those who are called, both Jews and Greeks, Christ the power of God and the wisdom of God. . . . But of Him you are in Christ Jesus, who became for us wisdom from God—and righteousness and sanctification and redemption. (1 Corinthians 1:24–30)

James has a lot to say on the subject of wisdom:

> Who is wise and understanding among you? Let him show by good conduct that his works are done in the meekness of wisdom. But if you have bitter envy and self-seeking in your hearts, do not boast and lie against the truth. This wisdom does not descend from above, but is earthly, sensual, demonic. For where envy and self-seeking exist, confusion and every evil thing are there. But the wisdom that is from above is first pure, then peaceable, gentle, willing to yield, full of mercy and good fruits, without partiality and without hypocrisy. (James 3:13–17)

We see there are two kinds of wisdom. One is demonic and one is from above, from God. Which one do you walk in? You can learn from this dream that it is not Jesus's desire to let you go. In fact, He will do all in His power to keep your hand in His. You must keep your heart in tune to His and allow Him to lead you past these temptations that seek to steal you away from Him.

> Keep me, O Lord, from the hands of the wicked; preserve me from violent men, who have purposed to make my steps stumble. (Psalm 140:4)

In the dream Jesus did not explain to me why He would not let me go to the desired object. He quietly led me His way. No explanation is needed when you trust Jesus. You are to learn to obey without question that His way is the right way for your life.

It is with a determined effort and prayer on your part that you can be so in step with Jesus that nothing can cause you to stumble.

> Therefore, brethren, be even more diligent to make your call and election sure, for if you do these things you will never stumble. (2 Peter 1:10)

What about you?
1. Do you trust Jesus with your life as the baby trusted his father not to drop him? If not, why not?

2. Has there been a time in your life where you quickly embraced something without thinking or asking God? What was the outcome?
3. Are you willing to place your hand in Jesus's hand and trust His leading? If not, what keeps you from doing this?

SECTION V
HOLY SPIRIT REVELATION

God gave the law originally as a railroad track to guide Israel's obedience. The engine that was supposed to pull a person along the track was God's grace, the power of the Spirit. And the coupling between our car and the engine was faith, so that in the Old Testament, like the New Testament, salvation was by grace, through faith, along the track of obedience (or sanctification).
—John Piper, author

CHAPTER 13

♥ LAW VERSUS SPIRIT

Dream: I was in a large room of a huge house set in the country. It seemed to be a banquet as there were many people present. The owner of the house was a well-dressed distinguished elderly lady, and I knew that I was somehow related to her. I was aware of her love for me. I was seated at a table across from the her along with six other people. Behind the lady stood a young man with dark hair who was quite tall—maybe seven feet or more. We knew each other. I was aware that he liked me as well as I liked him. Everyone was aware that there was a bad storm coming, but we continued to eat and drink and visit with each other enjoying ourselves. No one seemed to be concerned about the storm.

A messenger, an older man, was ushered into the room. He looked around, and when he saw me came to where I was seated. He told me that the sheriff sent him and wanted me to come stay with him so that he could protect me from the storm. The elderly lady smiled at him graciously and had the attendants give the man a plate of food so he could eat before he left to go back to the sheriff's office. I knew that the sheriff was also a man who liked me and was vying for my attention. As I pondered the sheriff's message, I looked at the tall, dark-haired man. He was still in his position behind the elderly lady. He knowing the dark-haired man did not want me to go, I playfully said to the sheriff's messenger, "Sure, I'll come with you." The dark-haired man was visibly disappointed and walked out of the room. I was surprised at his sudden action, and it caused me to ponder my decision. I questioned how I really felt. I knew both men liked me and wanted me to be with them.

At this point, I began to contemplate both men's attributes. I knew if I went with the sheriff I would be under his strict control and would no longer be free to be myself and that his intent was to take advantage of me. I also thought about the dark-haired man, and in my spirit I knew that he liked me, wanted the best for me, and that he was steadfast and true, as well as the fact that he would never press himself on me. I also knew that with him I would always be safe. I then realized that I wanted to stay with the dark-haired man and that I had hurt him tremendously by joking around.

I got up from the table and ran through the house looking for the dark-haired man hoping he had not left. I came to a large room where there were more people eating and enjoying themselves. I asked a young girl if she had seen the man. She said, "Yes, he's in that room in the hallway." There was a small room with the door shut. I could see light streaming under the door and could hear the man talking on the phone. I heard him say, "If you hurt her in any way you will answer to me." I knew he was talking to the sheriff. I waited in the next room for him to come out. While waiting, a young African American girl about five years old came to me and started talking about wearing a white robe. I explained to her what a white robe meant. She said her momma told her it was bad and that bad men wore white robes. I realized she was talking about the Ku Klux Klan. I explained to her that this was indeed bad but it was no longer happening. Now, wearing a white robe or white veil was a good thing. After talking to her, I went back to the small room. The door was open and I knew the man had left the room while I was talking to the child.

I walked back through the house trying to find the man again, hoping he had not left. I entered the banquet room where I had been at first and saw him again standing behind the elderly lady's chair. As I walked up to the table our eyes met, and I told him that I would like to talk to him. I could still see the disappointment in his eyes but also the love he had for me. I knew that he would not force me to choose him, but he had hoped that I would. I asked him to walk with me. We walked through the house and out onto the broad veranda. I turned and looked up at him saying, "I wanted to tell you that I am sorry I hurt you. I was teasing you, playing a game with you, and it was wrong. I'm not going with the sheriff. I'm staying right here."

He looked relieved. Then I said, "I want to say something that I hope you will want to hear. I love you." With that he smiled and embraced me.

As he started to give me a kiss I noted two men sitting in a car watching us. I thought to myself, maybe we shouldn't be so visible with affection then let it go and kissed the man lightly. We then walked back into the banquet room together. I saw the elderly lady look up at us and smile. She knew that I was staying there and had chosen wisely.

I noted that the man who came to bring me to the sheriff was still eating and enjoying himself. He did not want to go back to the sheriff himself and continued to sit there and eat. At this point, the two men who had been outside watching us came into the room. One of them grabbed my arm saying, "Come with us." I knew that my ex-husband sent them. I jerked my arm away and the dark-haired man stepped in front of me and said, "Take your hands off of her." With a quick move, one of the men hit him and he went down on the floor. I ran to stand behind the elderly lady. With authority she asked them what they wanted. One of the men said, "We've been sent to bring her back to her husband." I responded saying, "You tell him I am not coming back." The dark-haired man then stepped up and told them, "Get out. She doesn't belong to him anymore." The elderly lady demanded they leave her house, and they turned and walked out. The dark-haired man then turned and looked at me with such love I knew that I was where I belonged.

Truth: "For the law of the Spirit of life in Christ Jesus has made me free from the law of sin and death" (Romans 8:2).

This dream is symbolic of many Christians today who have been born again, received the atonement work of Christ, and yet still live under the law—under the legal system of religion. Just as the Pharisees and Sadducees lived by the letter of the law (or pretended they did), too often Christians, after being born again, begin to live by rules and regulations of a church with a works mentality instead of by faith. This is not the freedom Christ proclaimed for you to embrace.

Understand that I am not speaking against church here. I am speaking against rules and regulations of "do this, do that, or you cannot belong to this church." There was a reason Jesus preached in the market places and countrysides. He was not bound to man's idea of church or denomination. When any church goes strictly by man's rules and regulations, Jesus gets lost within the very church in which He is supposed to be glorified.

In this dream, I found myself in a house full of people enjoying themselves, relaxed, in fellowship with one another. This is symbolic of the true church (body of Christ) as well as our heavenly domain. I was seated at the table of the owner. The woman represents God. Behind her stood a man I admired whom I believe was Christ or the Holy Spirit. There was another man in the picture—the sheriff who represents the law. I liked both men. I was immature in my feelings as well as my knowledge of God's truth just as many Christians are immature in their faith and understanding of God's Word today.

You might be born again and never learn the truth of God, the ways of God, or even the love of God. Thus, you flit back and forth with the law (legalism in the church) and the Holy Spirit leading. You embrace the freedom Jesus offers and yet you adhere to the "traditions of men"—all in the name of church. Thus, you cannot overcome sin in your life because you are living by the law. You do not walk in the promised peace of God because you are pushed, pulled, and controlled by legalism. This is the immaturity, as well as lack of knowledge, that I displayed in my flirting around with the man. Your flesh will always gravitate toward the law. Paul confirms this in his letter to the Romans.

> For I delight in the law of God according to the inward man. But I see another law in my members, warring against the law of my mind, and bringing me into captivity to the law of sin which is in my members. O wretched man that I am! Who will deliver me from this body of death? I thank God—through Jesus Christ our Lord! So then, with the mind I myself serve the law of God, but with the flesh the law of sin. (Romans 7:22-25)

It is the Spirit of God who reveals truth to you that you may be delivered from the confines and bondage of the law—the legality of religious hierarchy.

After realizing how my wavering back and forth hurt the first man, I then looked within to see what I had done and question why I did it. I was given revelation for both sides. The Spirit of Truth desired that I follow Him, and the spirit of legalism demanded I follow it. One demands and one desires. As I weighed the two, I could see clearly and chose the right path. I then sought to make amends with the man/Spirit and let him know that I wanted to be with him, that I chose him, and that I was not going to adhere to the sheriff/law.

If you are not led by the Spirit of God, you grieve the Holy Spirit. He is real. He is the third person of the Trinity. Until you grasp and embrace the truth of the Holy Spirit, you will walk without the power of God in your life. Without the

Spirit, you are missing one-third of the full truth God has for you. In fact, you are quenching the Spirit of God.

> And do not grieve the Holy Spirit of God, by whom you were saved for the day of redemption. (Ephesians 4:30)

> Do not quench the Spirit. (1 Thessalonians 5:19)

Our arch enemy knows well that the law is an enticing trap. For centuries churches reigned by religious rules. It is not God's will that there be so many denominations in our culture. It is His will we have one church—the body of Christ—those who are true believers in Christ Jesus as Lord and Savior. However, because of likes, dislikes, personal selections, and/or prejudices, there will continue to be many denominations with their own thoughts and beliefs.

Jesus stands today offering you the kind of freedom you desire. The law, legalism, keeps you bound and in confusion of the reality of the freedom found only in Christ. This freedom is knowing who you are in Christ—knowing you are no longer under laws, rules, regulations, but in fact are able to freely worship without fear of making a mistake. The law brings death, and it is the strength of sin.

> The sting of death is sin, and the strength of sin is the law. (1 Corinthians 15:56)

Christ intended His church to be free to walk in love and fellowship and help one another, not tied to the old dictates of man. Paul stated that while he was lost he was under the traditions of his fathers.

> And I advanced in Judaism beyond many of my contemporaries in my own nation, being more exceedingly zealous for the traditions of my fathers. (Galatians 1:14)

Jesus addressed the Pharisees and Scribes when asked why his disciples did not walk according to the tradition of the elders:

> For laying aside the commandment of God, you hold the tradition of men—the washing of pitchers and cups, and many other such things you do. (Mark 7:5, 7)

This is the legal system in many churches today and in individuals who have not understood they are no longer under the law of sin and death. Legality lays aside the truth and freedom of Christ and demands its followers uphold traditions—denominations and non-denominations alike. Is church good? Yes, it is. Although it is true there must be order in the church, it is not to be a legal system to which we must adhere. Christ is to be revealed within the church, and we are to be free to worship Him.

In the dream I received revelation and quickly sought to confess my sin of riding the fence and not taking the Holy Spirit seriously. I repented and declared my love for Him. Before a kiss sealed the union, I resorted to the fear of man as I looked around to see if people were watching. Another form of legalism is a fear of what man will think when you fully embrace Christ and let it be known to all. This is your public announcement of professing Christ as well as following in baptism.

You, the bride of Christ, are to be chaste, loyal, and steadfast as you await His return. You are not to take lightly or play around with what Jesus did for you on the cross. He purchased you with His blood, setting you free from the curse of the law. You have been called to walk by faith in the light and truth of Christ Jesus and His act of love for you.

> Christ has redeemed us from the curse of the law, having become a curse for us (for it is written, "Cursed is everyone who hangs on a tree,") that the blessing of Abraham might come upon the Gentiles in Christ Jesus, that we might receive the promise of the Spirit through faith. (Galatians 3:13–14)

Do not be found unfaithful to the Holy Spirit by seeking to adhere to or include other teachings or doctrines. You are to grow in Christ and be grounded in the truth.

> Therefore, leaving the discussion of the elementary principles of Christ, let us go on to perfection, not laying again the foundation of repentance from dead works and of faith toward God, of the doctrine of baptisms, of laying on of hands, of resurrection of the dead, and of eternal judgment. (Hebrews. 6:1–2)

You are to have a firm foundation in the truth of God's Word.

> We should no longer be children, tossed to and fro and carried about with every wind of doctrine, by the trickery of men, in the cunning craftiness of deceitful plotting. (Ephesians 4:14)

> Holding fast the faithful word as he has been taught, that he may be able, by sound doctrine, both to exhort and convict those who contradict. (Titus 1:9)

You wait unfaltering for your bridegroom as you walk in the truth. It is only in this truth you are able to stand firmly and not be enticed to sin against the Spirit of God.

> Stand fast therefore in the liberty by which Christ has made us free, and do not be entangled again with the yoke of bondage. (Galatians 5:1)

Paul, in referring to Hagar (Abraham's concubine), called this act of Abraham and Hagar one of the flesh (the law), and he was told to cast out the flesh. By embracing Christ Jesus as Lord and Savior, you are a child of the promise. Isaac was the promised seed of Abraham (Galatians 4:28–31). In Galatians 3:19, Paul states that the law was added "because of transgressions, till the Seed should come to whom the promise was made." Again, you are no longer under the law of sin and death but under the spirit and life of Christ Jesus (see Romans 8:2).

In the end of this dream, some men came to bring me back to my old husband. I think you can guess who the old husband or master is: Satan himself. Before salvation, you served the law. You were under condemnation (see John

3:18). Once you receive Christ, you are no longer under Satan. You are blood-bought by Christ Jesus. Satan will try to get a foothold in your life even though you are now alive to Christ. There will be times when Satan will put up a fight for you, thinking he can demand you to come back to your old way of life by methods of shame, fear, and failing. You only need to remember to whom you now belong. Make sure your decision for Christ is solid. Satan has no authority over you once you claim Christ as your Savior.

It is time for the church to stop flirting with the law and the Spirit, the truth of God. You can have only one master and that choice, just as in the dream, is yours to make. The clarity of truth is revealed to you through God's Word. You choose it wisely, or you spurn it seeking the attentions of the world. Jesus will not force you to choose him. You must see the truth and embrace it for yourself.

> Now therefore, fear the Lord, serve Him in sincerity and in truth, and put away the gods which your fathers served on the other side of the River and in Egypt. Serve the Lord! And if it seems evil to you to serve the Lord, choose for yourselves this day whom you will serve, whether the gods which your fathers served that were on the other side of the River, or the gods of the Amorites, in whose land you dwell. But as for me and my house, we will serve the Lord. (Joshua 24:14–15)

Note that Joshua demanded the Israelites put away their foreign gods. The law can be a god to those who feel they must adhere to it. The Pharisees ritualistically adhered to the law, and thus, turned away from Jesus as Messiah. They could not have both. Joshua commands the Israelites to choose whom they will serve. You must mature in Christ and serve Him. The Bible warns of the consequences of being lukewarm, trying to serve both the world and God.

> I know your works, that you are neither cold nor hot. I could wish you were cold or hot. So then, because you are lukewarm, and neither cold nor hot, I will vomit you out of my mouth. (Revelation 3:15–16)

The law kills but the Spirit gives life.

> Not that we are sufficient of ourselves to think of anything as being from ourselves, but our sufficiency is from God, who also made us sufficient as ministers of the new covenant, not of the letter but of the Spirit; for the letter kills, but the Spirit gives life. (2 Corinthians 3:5-6)

The law is referred to as "the ministry of death" in 2 Corinthians 3:7. The law controls, binds, and causes stress, worry, and failure. The reason Christ came was because people could not keep the law. The law was good in that it revealed sin. After Christ came, who is the fulfillment of the law, you are no longer under the law—no longer serving the law. Do you still sin? Unfortunately, until Christ comes again, you do. However, sin should not be a pattern in your life. If you sin, you repent (stop sinning), you go on with Christ. The law is a stern taskmaster and is a controlling authority as the sheriff was in the dream. I knew he would be controlling and seemingly love me. But as I weighed the truth, I knew in my heart that the first man really cared about me, wanted good for me, and was steadfast and true. He did not ask me to choose nor try to persuade me. He just presented Himself as truth standing right before me.

Paul further states that if the law was glorious, "how will the ministry of the Spirit not be more glorious?" (2 Corinthians 3:8). If you follow Christ fully, you will no longer be tied to the law. You must see clearly where you are bound by the law, by men's traditions, and not the Word of God. Choose wisely whom you shall serve. When you begin to understand the revelation of freedom as Christ offers, you can easily choose the right path. You can be sure of your firm standing in Him.

> Therefore if the Son makes you free, you shall be free indeed. (John 8:36)

What about you?
1. Have you been in a situation of vacillating back and forth between two things? What was the outcome in your life?
2. Have you come to the place where you know how much God loves you? If not, what will you do to get to this place?
3. Have you been under the law of religion and not the Spirit of God? How will you change that?

One thing I have observed in all my years of ministry is that the most effective and important aspects of evangelism usually take place on an individual, personal level. Most people do not come to Christ as an immediate response to a sermon they hear in a crowded setting. They come to Christ because of the influence of an individual.
—John MacArthur, author

CHAPTER 14

♥ PROPHETIC EVANGELISM

Dream: My sister Teresa and I were walking up the side of a lush, green mountain. We stopped to take in the most breathtakingly beautiful mountainside of flowers that we'd ever seen, surrounding us where we stood as well as across the way on other mountains. In the dream, as we arrived at the top of the mountain, suddenly we were walking up the mountain again. It was the same scene as if God did a rewind! A double picture.

The second time as we got to the top there was a brick house to the right on the edge of a cliff. It appeared to be a one-story, simple brick house. Nothing fancy. I commented to my sister about it. She looked over and said, "It's okay. There's not much to it." I responded, "You have to see the back of it. It is built into the rock face of the mountain and has three stories with balconies. It is beautiful."

We walked on and saw a very exclusive resort built on the end of the cliff. There was an evangelist (one known in real life) and a young man with him standing under a large portico. They appeared to be waiting for us because they both walked forward to meet us. The four of us were then standing in an open clearing. We began talking and suddenly a small cloud (about three feet by four feet) descended down above us. With some trepidation, we stood in awe looking up at it. There was light pulsating from inside the cloud. I then saw two doves in the cloud facing one another and that the pulsating light was coming from them. In my excitement, I said, "It's the doves!" The cloud descended lower, and I had a strong desire to touch it. I reached up, and when I barely touched the cloud the two doves promptly flew into my chest. I gasped, surprised, and looked at the others with me.

The evangelist and the young man looked at me, and I could tell they were both surprised. The evangelist looked at the young man and questioned, "Why did she get it?" He had thought that he, as the evangelist, would receive the doves. The young man also seemed surprised but immediately turned from the evangelist and started speaking to me. I knew that he was telling me what this meant and what would happen in the future.

Truth: "If you abide in Me, and My words abide in you, you will ask what you desire, and it shall be done for you" (John 15:7).

When I awoke from this dream, I knew that God had spoken something to me and also that He had sealed those words in me. We find in Daniel that he was told to seal up the visions he had been given.

> And the vision of the evenings and mornings which was told is true; therefore seal up the vision, for it refers to many days in the future. (Daniel 8:26)

Some things are shown to us and then sealed for a later time in order to come to fruition in God's timing. Why sealed? I believe the Word that is sealed is active within the person while it remains sealed—preparing you for something that is to come but not allowing you to know as you may hinder the message, try to add your own thoughts and actions to it, or possibly, try to force the vision to happen.

I recall a young man being told by people he was God's man for the day. The people embraced him, well-known ministers and prophets embraced him, and people from all over the nations flocked to hear him. There was tremendous power in his meetings. The man quickly fell from grace with an act of adultery, ruining his ministry and his marriage. It was man who put this young man on a pedestal calling him to step out in ministry. He was so taken by the well-known people who endorsed him that he did as they said. The timing for this young man was not God's. It was man's. I've known of others who were extremely gifted and were told they needed to use their gift in ministry. They lasted a little while and shortly after burned out. Man's profuse flattery, exaltations, and urgings can be deadly to the person who is not listening to God. God's timing is essential in our walk with Him.

In this dream I felt it was a dream meant for me personally as well as for the church. It speaks of a double anointing of the Holy Spirit (two doves) having to do with evangelism. For clarity, please understand that there can be added anointings for certain tasks as you walk with Jesus.

At the beginning of the dream, walking up the mountain was replayed. In the prophetic world of numbers, the number two means confirmation. God confirmed this dream as a reality but only He knew the what, why, and when of it. Climbing higher is also symbolic of a higher walk with the Lord.

To this day, I still don't know what was said in this dream, only that for some reason I received the doves and not the others. If you desire Christ, reach out for Him, call to Him, and ask Him to be the Lord of your life. You will receive more from God than those who are apathetic toward God. You will be one of many Christians who are not ashamed of Jesus but will speak mightily with an anointing that is spoken into you as the words were spoken into me in this dream. Part of your receiving personally, as well as the church body's receiving, has to do with your reaching for whatever God has for you. It is a step of faith.

Note that in the dream I saw, with excitement, the doves being revealed. I seemed to know their purpose. I had a desire to touch them, whereas the others just watched. Maybe this is your desire today. You might be wondering if there is more to your life than there has been. I think all of us find ourselves in this holding pattern at some point as we go through seasons in our lives. Dull, dreary seasons do not mean God has left you; it means you are being taught. You are in a quiet, still place in order to hear, see, and know God. You are like a fine wine, being held until "such a time as this" (Esther 4:14).

Esther was in a position that she did not desire nor welcome. There came a time in her life when she was called on to do that for which God had positioned her. Because of her obedience she was able to save her people from genocide. You also go through seasons where you witness, teach, speak, and then find yourself in a dry, barren season. What you do with that time is important. First, ask God for clarification that you are where you are supposed to be and not out of His will. Then allow God to prune, cut, and shape you for the season to come. It is important that you believe God is in control. The Christian who seeks God continuously is always in His plan and will.

I believe this dream speaks clearly to those of you who are yearning for more, desiring to walk with God in a more powerful way. I also believe it is an assurance to you who have been waiting for a Word from God that God has not forgotten you. Until the day comes that you go home to be with Him, there is always more to do for the kingdom.

The plain house is symbolic of the simple, humble Christian who, by man's criteria, seems to be of no significance. In fact, Christians like this are passed over and not given the time of day in many instances. However, the house (though appearing simple and not worthy of a second glance) was embedded into the Rock (Jesus). The carnal man sees only plain and simple. The spiritual man sees beyond what is on the surface and into the depths of one's heart. It is this man or woman who will stand all storms of life and not be moved. Though they look simple and not someone thought of a as vibrant or highly learned, they have a solid footing in Christ.

> He is like a man building a house, who dug deep and laid the foundation on the rock. And when the flood arose, the stream beat vehemently against that house, and could not shake it, for it was founded on the rock. (Luke 6:48)

Likewise, Jesus tells us about the man who heard His words and does not do them.

> But he who heard and did nothing is like a man who built a house on the earth without a foundation, against which the stream beat vehemently; and immediately it fell. And the ruin of that house was great. (Luke 6:49)

The evangelist in the dream represents the office of the evangelist. The man is the Holy Spirit. The evangelist was one I know well. He spent many years in evangelism. He is symbolic of those who believe because they were gifted or were once gifted in a certain area, that they would likely be chosen to receive the anointing of added grace. This man expected the anointing to be given to him and it was not. There are those today who have been in ministry for years. Thus, they expect God to give them a special anointing when in fact they bear no humility or compassion for others. I know of a Bible teacher who was given a word by a young man who was new in receiving prophetic words. The Bible teacher took offense at such a novice giving him a word and said as much to the young man. About four years later that the Bible teacher and the young man's path crossed again. The teacher told him that his word had come true, not apologetically, but just acknowledged the man's word was true. You must beware of pride in your position and how long you have walked in your gift. Pride can be deadly, and no one is exempt from its intrusion. It is important to not become complacent in your gift or ministry. Allowing yourself to do so will dull your hearing and seeing in the Spirit.

The young man expected the evangelist to receive as well and was surprised. I am reminded of Samuel the priest and prophet when God told him to go to Jesse's house and anoint one of his sons as the next king (1 Samuel 16:1). Samuel thought he knew which son would be anointed as he was looking at the outward appearance. God had another criteria in mind.

> But the Lord said to Samuel, "Do not look at his appearance or at his physical stature, because I have refused him. For the Lord does not see as man sees; for man looks at the outward appearance, but the Lord looks at the heart." (1 Samuel 16:7)

We know in this story six sons passed before Samuel and not one of the six was God's choice. Samuel was puzzled. God had Samuel send for the youngest son who was out in the fields keeping sheep. He appeared and Samuel saw that he was young, had a ruddy complexion with bright eyes, and was good-looking. You might say he was the runt of the litter.

> And the Lord said, "Arise, anoint him; for this is the one!" (1 Samuel 16:12)

We know this was David, a humble shepherd boy who sang songs to God while he kept sheep, whom God Himself would say was a man after His own heart. David would not have been anointed king if it had been left up to Samuel the priest/prophet.

God is looking for the same humble hearts today, those who are after His heart. As in the dream in the chapter "Unconditional Love," where I handed God my heart and He handed me His, God wants to make your heart like His. He wants you to desire Him, to sit with Him in humility and patience waiting on Him. He wants you to stop making a comparison to what others are doing, to keep your hand to the plow, and to work in the field He has planted you for this season.

The two doves are symbolic of the Holy Spirit. As there were two, this confirms God's anointing for those whose hearts are looking toward Him. Do not think God has passed you by. You may be in training, some longer than others. In God's timing, He will say, "Go and do as I bid you."

Abraham was not a man the learned and elite would have chosen to be the father of all nations. But He is known as the father of faith. As we have faith, it is through Abraham that we are blessed.

> So then those who are of faith are blessed with believing Abraham. (Galatians 3:9)

Moses started his ministry at eighty years old. The first forty years of his life were spent in Pharaoh's palace having all riches. Accused of murder and debased, he ran for his life and spent forty years in the wilderness having nothing. Moses was written off by the world as dead. Yet, after forty years of wilderness living, God appeared to Moses and told him He had a job for him to do. "Come now, therefore, and I will send you to Pharaoh that you may bring My people, the children of Israel, out of Egypt" (Exodus 3:10). I believe God's thoughts were something like this: "Now he is ready. He has been stripped of himself and expects nothing."

Age is not a prerequisite for God to use you. He is not looking for youth and vigor. He is looking for a heart that is compliant to His hand. It is your faith and your heart God looks at. Ananias was a simple man, yet his name is recorded in the Bible as the man who brought God's Word and healing to Saul (Acts 9:10–18).

Are you in the wilderness today? Do you think God has forgotten about you? Not on your life. He knows exactly where you are. His timing is perfect for you. You are a harvester. You and those like you will rise up from all walks of life, young and old, small and great, to go forth to bring in the harvest, evangelizing in the areas around you. This should not be a surprise to anyone. Jesus' mandate was such as this.

> And Jesus came and spoke to them, saying, "All authority has been given to Me in heaven and on earth. Go therefore and make disciples of all the nations, baptizing them in the name of the Father and of the Son and of the Holy Spirit, teaching them to observe all things that I have commanded you; and lo, I am with you always, even to the end of the age." Amen. (Matthew 28:18-20)

In essence, Jesus said "I have all authority. I'm sharing that authority with you. I want you to go and witness (tell them about me) to the nations (wherever you are) and bring them into my kingdom of eternal life. I've appointed you as evangelists (harvesters), and there is plenty of harvesting to do of lost souls. Now, after you bring them into the kingdom of my Father, I want you to teach them my ways, everything I've said to you. Oh, and by the way, I'm going to be right alongside of you continually, helping you so you don't fail." It is Jesus who appoints us and equips us.

> After these things the Lord appointed seventy others also, and sent them two by two before His face into every city and place where He Himself was about to go. Then He said to them, "The harvest truly is great, but the laborers are few; therefore pray the Lord of the harvest to send out laborers into His harvest." (Luke 10:1-2)

Note that it was not just the twelve disciples who were sent out, but seventy others as well. How are you doing? Are you evangelizing, harvesting? Are you representing Jesus to others? Are you listening and obeying the Holy Spirit or refusing to go forth?

You are sealed with the Holy Spirit at the time of salvation. Along the way you may receive an additional filling or anointing as you grow in Christ through prayer, reading His Word, listening to God-ordained messengers. Your life should reflect Christ in all that you do and say. If you are on the wilderness side of life right now, don't give up. God has a plan and place for you. He is teaching you, growing you, and in His timing He will send you forth. Trust Him.

> So Jesus said to them again, "Peace to you! As the Father has sent Me, I also send you." (John 20:21)

What about you?
1. Have you sensed that God has something for you to do but you don't know what it is?
2. Are you in a dry season of your life? What are you doing while you go through this?
3. Have you been in a position like Esther when it was up to you to step out in faith in order for others to be saved? How did that make you feel?

God walls the sea with sand. God clears the air with storms. God warms the earth with snow. He exalts us to heaven by the stumbling-block of the cross.
Christopher Wordsworth, author

CHAPTER 15

♥ ENCOUNTERING STUMBLING BLOCKS

Dream: I was driving an eighteen-wheeler down a country road with the trailer full of food. I seemed to be in a hurry to get somewhere. I saw ahead of me stones in the road, but also noted quickly that though they were huge—about one foot by four feet long—they were smooth and flat. I did not stop but kept driving and drove right on top of the flat stones, continuing to my destination. I came to a place where the road curved to the right, and as I rounded the curve, before me were huge boulders about three to five feet in diameter strewn throughout the roadway blocking my way. I came to a complete stop. I knew I could not drive over these stones. I got out of the truck and started lifting the boulders and throwing them off the road. There was a low bridge in front of me which I had to drive under.

As I was removing the boulders, a man came down from the hill with a shotgun. He pointed it at me and said, "This is my road and you are not going any farther." I stood there silent. I was not afraid. I knew I was not going to turn around and go back. I looked to my right, and three men were coming down the hill on the opposite side of the road. I knew they were angels of the Lord. I watched as the men called the man over and talked with him. After a moment the man returned and apologized to me and said that I could go on through. The three men started removing the boulders as the man left. It got in the truck and went on through to my destination.

Truth: "For the weapons of our warfare [are] not carnal but mighty in God for pulling down strongholds, casting down arguments and every high thing that exalts itself against the knowledge of God, bringing every thought into captivity to the obedience of Christ" (2 Corinthians 10:4–5).

This dream speaks of stumbling blocks, which are found in all walks of life. These are the things that cause you to stumble in your Christian walk. All stumble, but do all get up and go on with the Lord?

Note that I was driving a large truck full of food. This is provision for many people. I was in a hurry to get where I was headed. These are the apostles, prophets, evangelists, pastors, and teachers who carry the Word of God to nations everywhere. As an individual, you also carry God's Word to those around you in your place of ministry. You will always encounter obstacles to your efforts, especially when Jesus is mentioned, because it is the nature of Satan to stop the Word of God and the name Jesus from being shared.

The first obstacle was intended to stop me. However, I pressed forward, seeing that I was able to drive over the blockage and continue on my path. What was meant to be a barrier did not stop nor slow me down. There are situations in your life where you know what to do and how to do it from your years of experience of being led by the Holy Spirit, and you keep going. You know to go to prayer and read the Word. Thus you find the strength to keep going and do not give heed to things trying to halt your progress.

The second blockage was one that halted my progress. It was not something I could ignore and keep moving forward. It was something that would take some time to remove. There are circumstances where you cannot always move ahead immediately as the remedy may take some time. I thought I could move the stones, but in my efforts I encountered another hindrance to my efforts. The man! He can represent Satan as well as people in your life who keep you from moving on with God. There are times when stuff happens in your life, unexpected stuff, and you are kept from going forward. No matter what you attempt in the flesh, you encounter one closed door after another and cannot seem to move forward. However, if you are prepared for such times, you can rest assured that you will continue on your path as you wait on God.

Nehemiah was sent to rebuild the walls of Jerusalem. We read his story in the book of Nehemiah. Nehemiah heard the report that the walls of his beloved Jerusalem were broken down and the gates were burned with fire. He heard how the people were in bondage to their enemies and to elements of the world. He was so grieved that he fell weeping for his people, his nation. He fasted and prayed for three months. Then, and only when he was Spirit led, He went before the king bearing his cup of wine. The king, noticing Nehemiah's sorrow of heart, questioned him as to the reason for his countenance. Though Nehemiah feared the king he spoke the truth as led by the Holy Spirit. He told the king of his sorrow and heaviness of heart for his people and for Jerusalem. In God's timing, after Nehemiah fasted and prayed, God gave Nehemiah favor with the king so the king allowed him to go and rebuild Jerusalem's walls. Nehemiah faced a roadblock. He saw a need but could not do anything about it. After he waited on God and prayed and fasted, the doors opened for him to go forward. Not only did the king grant him permission to leave, the king also provided all the timber needed to rebuild the gates of the walls as well as for houses. This was the hand of God.

Nehemiah is a perfect example of how your attitude should be in any situation. Each time the enemy (through the guise of man or friend) came to speak discouragement and threats to Nehemiah, the Word states, "Nehemiah prayed to the Lord." He did not waste words or time with any enemy. He turned to God, prayed, and continued the work God sent him to accomplish. Even the people building the wall were alert to their enemy and were not found asleep in their mission.

> Those who built on the wall, and those who carried burdens, loaded themselves so that with one hand they worked at construction, and with the other held a weapon. (Nehemiah 4:17)

The book of Nehemiah is a fascinating story of favor, trust, and waiting on God. Remember Nehemiah when burdens weigh you down or roadblocks bring you to a halt, and make it a point to fast and pray to the Lord. It is He who provides the answers you need as well as the strength to carry through. Prayer is vital to every Christian.

The man with the shotgun is, of course, those who would stop the spread of the gospel of Jesus Christ—unbelievers and mockers of God, and especially of Christ Jesus as Messiah. The man in my dream is symbolic of many who do not want anything to do with the church or religion and will not allow it, as far as it is in their control, to be spoken of or given to others. We have people like this today, and we can see our world becoming more and more anti-God.

Before retirement, my husband Jimmy worked with a group of younger adults with whom he got along with very well. There was one young man who walked in a perverse lifestyle and made it a point to talk about his church and God in front of everyone. He seemed to butt heads with Jimmy at times over the issues they discussed. There was a discussion one day about people being anti-God. Jimmy stated that most people will allow you to speak of God, but it is when you mention the name Jesus they get very upset. Jimmy said the young man was listening, along with some others. Before this conversation, this man usually rebuked everything Jimmy said, but this time he did not. With amazement, he commented, "You are right!" as if he were realizing this for the first time. Jimmy said he knew by the man's expression that he saw truth that day. I don't know what happened to this young man, but I do know that he heard, saw, and embraced a seed of light and truth that day. I believe God will use that seed to remove stumbling blocks from his path.

Today you work in and for the kingdom as well as carry the burdens of others in prayer. You should never find yourself without God's weapons—the blood of Christ covering you (salvation) and the sword of the Spirit, which is the Word of God (Ephesians 6:17). You should be assured you belong in the kingdom of God. You need to be spiritually alert to the enemy around you that you might give warning to the body of Christ.

In the John chapter 15, Jesus begins telling the disciples of certain things that would happen and not to be surprised when they do. He then tells them that He is sending them the Helper, the Spirit of Truth, the Holy Spirit, who will testify of Jesus. Jesus follows up with why He is telling them all these things.

> These things I have spoken to you, that you should not be made to stumble. (John 16:1)

Have you ever thought that you can be *made* to stumble? You might have thought about your stumbling as your fault. But there are times when stumbling blocks are before you designed by your enemy Satan. Jesus was telling the disciples that if they knew the truth, knew these things will happen, they wouldn't be caught unaware or made to stumble because of unbelief or ignorance. They would be able to stand strong in the light and truth of Christ.

Peter also spoke about stumbling:

> Therefore, brethren, be even more diligent to make your call and election sure, for if you do these things you will never stumble; for so an entrance will be supplied to you abundantly into the everlasting kingdom of our Lord and Savior Jesus Christ. (1 Peter 1:10-11)

Diligent is a powerful word. If you are diligent in making sure your salvation is intact, not just head knowledge, but heart change, you will never stumble. Sounds too good to be true, doesn't it? Peter follows with the assurance that if you make sure you are abiding in Christ and He in you (which is how you can be sure of your salvation), not only will an entrance into the kingdom of God be provided for you, but an abundant entrance. A wide open, large, plentiful, rich entrance.

There are many ways to stumble. Here are three: (1) sometimes spiritual forces are at work in your life and, through no fault of your own, stumbling blocks are set before you; (2) other times, because you have been lax in reading God's Word and spending time in prayer, ensuring your union with Christ is right and tight, you stumble because of your own negligence; and (3) you can be a stumbling block to someone else's faith or salvation by failing to live as Christ tells you. What you do and say speaks loudly to those who watch you. You are commanded to love your brethren, and this is by action and word. John states that if you fail to adhere to Jesus's word to love your brethren, you might stumble.

> He who loves his brother abides in the light, and there is no cause for stumbling in him. (1 John 2:10)

Stumbling is not pleasant no matter what the cause. When you are facing a dilemma, do as Nehemiah did. Fast and pray. God will affirm Himself to you. You will know what to do, and you will be back on track with God.

We talked about how to avoid stumbling blocks, but let's look at one place where you *should* stumble. It is a stumbling stone you should fall over and lay prostrate before until you see the revelation of the truth of God, the light of Christ, and are filled with the Holy Spirit. This is the cross of Jesus Christ. Until you stumble over this stone, you will never know the full truth of God's love and plan for your life.

There are promises of God that give you hope and help you stand strong in times of turmoil; hope that you can overcome those rocks in your pathway; hope that your salvation is safe and you need not fear anything that comes your way. I'm sure that you have met hurdles in your lives. Some you handle and keep going. With others, you scream, rant, rave, and fall apart. You must trust God in all things.

In this dream, the man purposefully set the boulders in the roadway to stop all progress and provision being taken to the people. How many churches today are coasting, barely getting by, as there is no abundant provision for the sheep? They are spiritually dying, or stagnant. They need the life of Christ to stir them up. How many churches function without Jesus? You might think that's impossible. Is it? When a church becomes man's ideas and visions and not God's, Jesus is not glorified and the Holy Spirit cannot do much work there.

> Now He did not do many mighty works there because of their unbelief. (Matthew 13:58)

In this passage Jesus was in his own home country—the place where He grew up. Those whom he had known all his life did not believe in Him. Jesus is always a gentleman and will in no way push Himself on you.

After the three men in the dream who were angels spoke to the man, speaking the truth of Christ to him, the man saw the error of his ways, repented, and apologized for his behavior. This is symbolic of the Holy Spirit removing the hardness from the man's heart. The man's heart was no longer hardened, and he was willing to allow the provision to go forward. God wants your heart. He wants to give you a new spirit and a new heart, a heart of flesh and not of stone.

> Then I will give them one heart, and I will put a new spirit within them, and take the stony heart out of their flesh, and give them a heart of flesh, that they may walk in My statutes and keep My judgments and do them; and they shall be My people, and I will be their God. (Ezekiel 11:19-20)

The provision being carried is the full provision of God. This is the authority, gifts, signs, miracles, wonders, and tongues that God has ordained for the church, the body of believers. There are churches today that have not allowed the fullness of God, as His Word states, to come into their church. Provision is there, but it has been blocked from being received by the very authorities who are over the people. It is your constant prayer for the body of Christ, as was Nehemiah's, which will allow God to send His Spirit to speak to the hearts of the pastors and individuals who block God's fullness. How our Lord Jesus must weep because of those who call themselves Christian (followers of Christ) and yet fail to know the fullness of His authority that is available to them. Only as the church is allowed full provision of the Word and gifts of God, can it rise up to be a body truly in unity and truth in Christ.

Only in trusting Christ can you go forward and overcome every hindrance, every obstacle, and every spirit that seeks to cause you to stumble. As you are the victor then you can help others who are waiting to hear the revelation of Christ Jesus. This is the provision you carry.

What about you?

1. Have you identified stumbling blocks in your life? What will you do about them?
2. Has your life ever caused someone else to stumble? What did you do about it?
3. Do you have family members with whom you find it hard to share the gospel? How do you handle that?

To learn strong faith is to endure great trials. I have learned my faith by standing firm amid severe testings.
—George Mueller, author

CHAPTER 16

♥ STANDING STRONG IN FAITH

Throughout the world we will always have trials and tribulations. (John 16:33)

In April 2011, devastating tornados wreaked havoc here in our home state of Alabama. They bore the fruit of John's "trials and tribulations." In the blink of an eye, many lives were lost and many towns and communities were destroyed. We live in a fallen world and one in which Satan has been given control by man's sin. In other words, "Things happen." We reside in an imperfect world and we are imperfect people (yes, even as Christians we are imperfect). Which one of us can say we are holy and have no sin? As we dwell deeper and deeper in Christ, in His Word, in His very presence, we are able to stand stronger and stronger, but only as we dwell steadfastly.

If we keep our eyes on the storm, on the devastation, on the trauma, we see only bad. If we keep our eyes on our stronghold Jesus, we can see how to pray, how to help, how to keep standing. Paul tells us in the Ephesians, "And having done all, to stand." You might ask, Done all of what? Ephesians 6:10-13 tells us:

> Finally, my brethren, be strong in the Lord and in the power of His might. Put on the whole armor of God, that you may be able to stand against the wiles of the devil. For we do not wrestle against flesh and blood, but against principalities, against powers, against the rulers of the darkness of this age, against spiritual hosts of wickedness in the heavenly places. Therefore take up the whole armor of God, that you may be able to withstand in the evil day, and having done all, to stand.

Paul says first be strong in God and in God's power. Your relationship should be such that there is no doubt as to who God is and what He has done for you. Then you are to put on the whole armor of God. Paul explains why you should do this—because you are in a spiritual battle. If you are not spiritually strong in God, you will fail. He then tells you how to stand in the full armor of God as well as what each piece of armor is:

> Stand therefore, having girded your waist with truth, having put on the breastplate of righteousness, and having shod your feet with the preparation of the gospel of peace; above all, taking the shield of faith with which you will be able to quench all the fiery darts of the wicked one. And take the helmet of salvation, and the sword of the Spirit, which is the word of God; praying always with all prayer and supplication in the Spirit, being watchful to this end with all perseverance and supplication for all the saints. (verses 14–18)

Paul urges you as if he were pleading with you to listen. Do this! You must do this! He shows you how to gird yourself with the truth of God, His Word, as you walk in the righteousness of God having prepared yourself in and with the Word of God to witness to all you meet.

Then Paul speaks two words: "Above all"! Above all of this preparation, you are to take up, believe, embrace faith. You can have all the other requirements, but without faith your works are simply works. Your fighting is only fighting in the flesh, and you will lose the battles that you cannot escape. Unless you have faith and believe God, you are simply a person clad in a suit of armor all the while trembling in fear and unable to go forward to battle. It is faith that moves mountains (see Matthew 17:20; 20:21). It is faith that caused Abraham to go out from his family and follow a God he did not know. It was faith that carried the saints of old in the footsteps of God, and they did not fear where He led them. Chapter 11 of Hebrews is the great faith hall of fame. Read it and find out what it was that spurred these followers of God onward in the midst of the unknown, of devastation, catastrophes, and loss.

Likewise, as a Christian you must do all in order to be able to stand firm in God, in faith. As a baby, you learned to walk by sporadically testing your legs and in the process received many a bump and bruise. The more you got up to try—and not lay down and quit—the stronger your legs became, until you are now grown into them and can walk upright for long periods of time with much strength. It is true also of your spiritual walk. You grow up into Christ.

> That we should no longer be children tossed to and fro . . . [and] may grow up in all things into Him who is the head—Christ. (Ephesians 4:14–15)

Many know this, yet somehow fail to see it. Do you ever ask, What is wrong? Why do I keep failing? Why doesn't God help me? God has given you the Way, the Truth, and the Life (John 14:6), and yet you insist there must be another safer, easier way. In other words, you insist on trying to do things your way! Self's desires will constantly battle against Christ. Choosing self over God's Word is an open door to the enemy of your soul, who seeks all whom he may devour (1 Peter 5:8).

When you refuse the whole truth of God, you have purposefully cracked the door open for entrance of the god of this world. You cannot have it both ways. You must determine to stop, listen, and obey what God is speaking to you. Stop seeking to feel good, to pick and choose what you want to do or where you want to go and the way to do so. There is still but one way to come out ahead in life and that is through Christ Jesus.

> If anyone loves me he will keep My Word; and My Father will love him, and We will come to him and make Our home with him. (John 14:23)

Obedience to the Word of God and not to yourself is the key to all things you need in your life. First His presence, then daily needs. "Seek first the kingdom of God and his righteousness, and all these things shall be added to you" (Matthew 6:33).

What things? The things you need: food, clothes, drink, peace of mind, and comfort to those of you who mourn. All things come from God and He has revealed to you how to access them. Seek Him first. Seek Jesus fully. Once you understand that your life, which is no longer of this world, (see John 15:19) belongs to God and those needs can only be met by God, you can turn to Him with full expectation. You must remember that you came to Christ Jesus asking Him to be Lord of your lives. Do you dare take that life back and cause His Lordship to be null and void in your life? Be careful that you do not allow fear to supersede your faith by choosing to believe God cannot do something in your life.

> He is able to do exceedingly abundantly above all we ask or think. (Ephesians 3:21)

God not only hears you but goes beyond what you ask for abundantly more than you ask. You ask for simple, earthly things that you see. God wants to give you the real life, the things of the spiritual world that cause you to see Him, hear Him, spend time with Him, and stand strong with and for Him. That is our Father God's love for you.

The problem lies in the fact that you still have one foot in the world and one with God. You are divided. You hear the liar (Satan) whisper that God's Word does not work, just as he whispered doubt about God to Eve. Indeed, God's Word cannot work if you cling to the world's goods and ways, accepting Satan's offerings. Faith is the key to anything you ask of God. Without faith you are like a divided soul wandering around in confusion not knowing what to believe.

James 1:5-8 addresses this dilemma. The writer clearly says not to expect an answer from God if you doubt God. He states that if you doubt, you are like a wave tossed to and fro by the wind. Faith and doubt cannot, and will never be able to, walk hand in hand. You must ask God to cleanse your spirit, mind, and begin a new walk in the truth in faith. You must stop looking at the circumstances. Don't allow depression to overtake you. If circumstances are not to your liking, do you hide your head, cry, moan and groan, and shut your Lord out? In this scenario, you only dig a deeper hole. You must stop withdrawing into self, look up, and hang onto Christ in praise, adoration, love, and faith. Christ set you free so look up with faith and not down in despair. If you feed your faith you will starve doubt.

Start with praise today! No matter what is going on in your life, praise God. Note, I did not say praise God for the bad things. Again I say, "Praise God" for who He is, that He is, and for who He will always be.

A preacher I mentioned earlier, Maria Woodworth-Etter, lost five out of her six children. One by one, they died either as infants or before age seven. Only one lived. Maria praised God through each death. Yes, she mourned, cried, and was sorrowful. But she praised God for His wisdom and knew she would see her children again. She had faith that though her children were not allowed a life here on earth, they would be waiting for her in the heavenly kingdom.

Life happens to all of us. Whatever your circumstances today, let your focus and faith be on God in spite of the storm. Only as you praise God can you begin to see beyond the storm. Only as you cling to God can you receive the nourishment, comfort, and peace you so badly need at times. Only in standing firm in God's Word can you stand in faith and rebuke doubt, casting it out. God's Word is like a daily vitamin C. Only as you determinedly "put on" Christ every day can you be healthy, whole, and strong. This is how you build up your faith and immunity from the sickness of this world. Do you believe this? In believing, purpose to stand today. Stand up, shake off the lies and the false beliefs, and cling to Christ. He is your only hope. He is the strength of your life. He is the comfort of your soul. He is your faith! And having done all this, you will stand!

What about you?

1. Have you been through a devastating event where your total trust had to be in God? What was the outcome?
2. Do you find yourself relying on your own strength to get through things? If so, how will that change in your life?
3. Has there been a time in your life when you praised God in spite of the storm and refused to be moved by fear? How did that change your life?

The doctrines of the gospel are meant to mould us so that our lives begin to "set" in the likeness of Christ. We have made little or no impression upon the world, for the very reason that the gospel doctrine has made a correspondingly slight impression upon us. It cannot be overemphasized that men and women who have accomplished anything in God's strength have always done so on the basis of their grasp of truth.
—Sinclair B. Ferguson, author

CHAPTER 17

♥ IN GOD'S STRENGTH

Dream: In this dream I was seated on the right side of a man. I could not see him nor did I know who he was, only that he was there. He was speaking to me, giving me instructions for something he wanted me to do. I don't know what the instructions were, only that he spoke it to me and caused fear to come over me. I thought, *I can't do that. I don't have the strength*. I did not speak this out loud to the man, only thought it. I then turned to the man and said, "Please, wait a moment. I will be right back." I went out of that room to another room. When I came back into the room I sat down and said to the man, "Okay, I'll do it. I have the strength I need now."

Truth: "It is God who arms me with strength, and makes my way perfect" (Psalm 18:32).

In this dream I was told to do something by a man with no name or face. Usually when this happens it is the Holy Spirit. He is our teacher, our helper, who is not only with us but dwells in us. When told the task that I was to do I was afraid as I knew in myself that I could not do what was being asked of me. By not saying no to the man's request, I knew it was something God wanted me to do. However, my immediate inward reaction was *I* can't do that. A carnal reflex. I quickly went out of the presence of the man to pray and be alone with God. I received the strength of God (or *power*, which is another word for strength) that I needed to do the task. Then, and only then, after I knew I had received God's strength, did I go back and accept the task given to me.

It is only in God's strength that you can accomplish what you are called to do. If you attempt to do something in your flesh it will fail. You might often wonder why something did not happen the way you planned, and this may well be the reason. *You* planned. As you learn to wait upon God, He will supply the strength you need in any situation He purposes in your life. You will then always go forth in obedience to His calling.

This dream is a reminder that God may call you to tasks that you feel inadequate to fill (and you are in the physical realm). You may enter into situations in which you have no confidence. If you will first draw away with God in prayer and seek Him for His strength to fulfill the mission, you can readily accept the task put before you. A personal example is writing this book. I feel inadequate and lack confidence. Yet it is He who keeps spurring me on, strengthening me, giving me words to write. What a wonderful Abba Father we have that He not only calls us to tasks He has appointed us to carry out, but fills us with His strength to accomplish and complete the task. Is there any question that He gets all the glory?

It is God who supplies you with the fuel (His Word, strength, peace, love, and faith) to travel the path He sets before you. In this way He receives the glory due Him, and you cannot boast of what you did. Paul boasted in his infirmities, his weaknesses, not in pride or strength of his own.

> Therefore most gladly I will rather boast in my infirmities, that the power of Christ may rest upon me. (2 Corinthians 12:9)

> Paul knew who saved him, who changed him, and the power that filled him was not his own.

> But God forbid that I should boast except in the cross of our Lord Jesus Christ, by whom the world has been crucified to me, and I to the world. (Galatians 6:14)

> A few reminders of the strength of our lives:

> The Lord is my rock and my fortress and my deliverer; My God, my strength, in whom I will trust; My shield and the horn of my salvation, my stronghold. (Psalm 18:2)

> For You have armed me with strength for the battle; You have subdued under me those who rose up against me. (Psalm 18:39)

Let the words of my mouth and the meditation of my heart be acceptable in Your sight, O Lord, my strength and my Redeemer. (Psalm 19:14)

The Lord is my strength and my shield; My heart trusted in Him, and I am helped; Therefore my heart greatly rejoices, And with my song I will praise Him. (Psalm 28:7)

In any situation you are facing, determine to first seek God for direction, confirmation, and the strength to go forward, and you will find yourself able to walk in any circumstance to which He calls you. If He calls you to it, He will supply you with the strength to do it.

He who calls you is faithful, who also will do it. (1 Thessalonians 5:24)

What about you?

1. Have you ever been asked to do something you knew you could not do, but you trusted God and were able to complete the assignment? How did you feel?
2. Do you seek God in prayer for all things? If not, why not?
3. Is God the first person you turn to in any situation? If not, what will you do to change that?

SECTION VI
WHEN CHRIST RETURNS

Many, I fear, would like glory, who have no wish for grace. They would [want to] have the wages, but not the work; the harvest, but not the labor; the reaping, but not the sowing; the reward, but not the battle. But it may not be.
—J. C. Ryle, author

CHAPTER 18

♥ THE END-TIME HARVEST

Vision: I was sitting on the right side of Jesus by a narrow, shallow stream. We were dangling our feet in the water, both of us laughing and playing, splashing the water with our feet. I was a child of about twelve. Suddenly, Jesus rose up and started across the stream stepping on stones. Thinking He was leaving me, I stood up and said, "Wait for me." He turned and chuckled, holding his left hand out to me, and said, "Come." I put my hand in His, and we crossed over the stream. We walked along the stream's bank, which was only wide enough for one person at a time. I followed behind Jesus. This pathway had the stream on one side and a mountain rising straight up on the other. I asked, "Where are we going?" He replied, "To the other side." I looked up at the mountain, and asked, "Are we going around this mountain?" He replied, "No. We're going through it." I was puzzled as the mountain was very high and seemed to be endless.

I continued to follow Jesus taking note of the water and the mountain. I glanced up again at the mountain, and when I looked back Jesus had disappeared. I started to panic but walked a few steps and came to a crevice in the mountain. I could see Jesus walking through the crevice so I followed him. As we neared the end of the crevice, I could see light ahead. As I stepped out into the light, I looked around and gasped, "Oh!" Before us, as far as the eye could see, was a field of ripe, golden wheat, ready to be harvested. There was one huge tree dominating the middle of the field as if watching over it. I was excited and turned to Jesus and said, "You go and get the others, and I'll start cutting wheat." I had a machete in my hand and began to cut wheat. I saw that Jesus was beside me and He also was cutting wheat. Thinking He had gone to get others to come help, I said to Him, "What about the others?" He laughed his beautiful laugh and said, "They'll come."

Truth: "Then He said to them, 'The harvest truly is great, but the laborers are few; therefore pray the Lord of the harvest to send out laborers into His harvest'" (Luke 10:2).

This is undoubtedly one of my fondest visions. It brought such joy and peace to me and still does today. I was as a child with a child's heart, and I was with Jesus.

> Assuredly, I say to you, whoever does not receive the kingdom of God as a little child will by no means enter it. (Mark 10:15)

I distinctly remember the joy I felt and the laughter and ease of being with Jesus. I so enjoyed His laughter with me as well as at me. It is a picture of who Jesus is, and few know Him this way. The beginning was a time of playing and intimacy with Jesus, trusting Him enough to follow wherever He was leading me. I didn't care where we went. I just wanted to be with Him.

> To everything there is a season, A time for every purpose under heaven . . . a time to plant, and a time to pluck what is planted . . . and a time to laugh. (Ecclesiastes 3:1–4)

As we crossed over the stream, we were crossing into another season in my life. We had first been playing. Now we were going somewhere else. The mountain represents an obstacle that appears insurmountable and would normally keep anyone from their destination. The human eye would see no way around it; thus, they quit. Have you ever encountered an obstacle in your life's path that seemed to be too much and you gave up before you arrived at your intended destination? Only by following Jesus's lead can you press on and go through any hindrance into your next season. The harvest is ready. Ripe golden wheat is as far as the eye can see. The harvest in our world is more than we can encompass in our carnal mind. Today, there are hundreds of thousands of souls who are still lost who do not know Christ Jesus as Lord and Savior.

The tree represents God. The one true living God is the "Lord of the harvest" (Matthew 9:38; Luke 10:3). Workers are desperately needed. Note that in this vision I immediately set to work harvesting, expecting Jesus to bring more to share in the work. Why did He not leave? Because though He is with you where you are, He is also with others who belong to Him.

> Let your conduct be without covetousness; be content with such things as you have. For He Himself has said, "I will never leave you nor forsake you." (Hebrews 13:5)

The quote above from Hebrews is about moral direction in our lives. When you accept Christ as your Lord and Savior, you become one with Him. Your conduct and contentment are found only in Him. When you are about Jesus's work, He comes alongside you as you work for and with Him. You allow Him to lead you in that work, knowing He will not leave you.

Note also that He led me to the harvest, and I was the only one harvesting. Why? Jesus stated it as a matter of fact:

> Then He said to His disciples, "The harvest truly is plentiful, but the laborers are few. Therefore pray the Lord of the harvest to send out laborers into His harvest." (Matthew 9:37–38)

This dream is still the cry of Jesus's heart. "The workers are few." As a Christian, you are all called to be an end-time harvester. Some have mightily fulfilled this position and have now gone on to their eternal home. Some are busily at work today bringing in a harvest of souls. Sadly, however, far too many are doing nothing except waiting. They received their salvation through faith in Jesus but refuse to work in and for the kingdom of God. Jesus's words above should be a revelation to you that the laborers are still very few. You must harvest continuously, knowing our Lord will give you rest beside the stream of peace when needed. You also need to pray for laborers to enter into the harvest with you. Jesus is with the harvesters today and will be with those who come forth to harvest.

Too often, Christians want the benefits Christ gives while adhering to their own direction and desires in life. Some desire Christ as a passenger in their vehicle/ministry, while others want Him relegated to the backseat to speak only when needed. Christ cannot give you instruction or direction when you refuse to walk in His commandments and allow Him to lead. You must desire and pursue Him that you may walk in His purposes and will for your life. It is only then that you can embrace peace that can pass your mental understanding (see Philippians 4:6) and your countenance is lifted to see clearly the way you should go. In Christ alone can you be certain to find your way.

> Jesus said to him, "I am the way, the truth, and the life. No one comes to the Father except through Me." (John 14:6)

Do not be deceived, my friends. There is no other way to God except through Christ Jesus. Part of your harvesting is helping others know this truth. Christ is Messiah! Christ alone can save! There are many religions today that offer eternity without Christ, and it is the greatest deception there is, for its fruit is eternal separation from God. Without Christ Jesus there is no heavenly eternity. You are all called to be a harvester—to be Christ to someone else. It is not God's will that any should perish.

> The Lord is not slack concerning His promise, as some count slackness, but is longsuffering toward us, not willing that any should perish but that all should come to repentance. (2 Peter 3:9)

Because of His great love, Father God extends the time for all. God has given you His Word to know truth and error. Unless you read it (His love letter to you) and allow the Holy Spirit to reveal truth to you, you will not be able to comprehend the error of your ways nor help someone else come to this truth. On the other hand, if you know the truth, then indeed you have been set free by the truth:

> Then Jesus said to those Jews who believed Him, "If you abide in My word, you are My disciples indeed. And you shall know the truth, and the truth shall make you free." (John 8:31-32)

Jesus's word gives you the light of truth to walk by. You are His hands, feet, voice, and most importantly, His love to all you encounter. Consider the many people you have met in your life and could have witnessed to and failed because you were too busy serving your own desires, habits, and addictions.

All have failed in this manner at one time or another. However, today is a new day. "The truth shall set you free." Today you can get busy and begin listening to our Lord, be led by the Holy Spirit, and cause someone to be snatched from the very fires of hell itself and planted in the kingdom of God. If you know God, you know love. If you know love, you cannot stand by idly watching others fall into the depth of eternal damnation.

> And on some have compassion, making a distinction; but others save with fear, pulling them out of the fire, hating even the garment defiled by the flesh. (Jude 22–23)

You witness to some through compassion and kindness; to others you witness as if you were snatching them from the pit of hell—the eternal death. You are to hate the sin but must witness to and love the sinner. Just as you were once lost and now are found, was blind but now see, there are countless who are still lost and blind. By God's mercy and grace you were pulled out of the mire and set on holy ground before Him through Christ. His blood atonement granting eternal life with Abba Father was accomplished for you.

Jesus wants you to spend time with Him. "Come and rest and splash your feet in the water with Me" is His offer. He wants you to follow Him, harvesting where He leads. What are you doing to ensure that those around you know this life with Christ? Revealing Christ to others should not be taken lightly. It is a matter of life and death.

What about you?

1. Have you felt the joy and ease of Jesus in your life? If not, how will you rectify that?
2. Has there been a task given to you where you refused it as you felt it was too much for you? How did you feel?
3. Are you harvesting today right where you are? What is holding you back?

Very soon the shadow will give way to Reality. The partial will pass into the Perfect. The foretaste will lead to the Banquet. The troubled path will end in Paradise. A hundred candle-lit evenings will come to their consummation in the marriage supper of the Lamb. And this momentary marriage will be swallowed up by Life. Christ will be all and in all. And the purpose of marriage will be complete.
—*John Piper, author*

CHAPTER 19

♥ THE WEDDING DANCE

Dream: I was in a place that I would call a heavenly atmosphere. I was dressed in the most beautiful, full-length ball gown. Its color was as a pearl shimmering in light. It had a full skirt with elbow-length sleeves. The bodice was slightly low at the neck but not revealing. (The gown reminded me of some of the gowns that Deborah Kerr wore as Anna in the movie *The King and I*. This is my all-time favorite movie, and I have long admired her gowns, so I am not surprised at the choice of gown in this dream.)

I was standing still as Jesus walked up to me. He put His right hand lightly on my back as I placed my left hand on His shoulder. I placed my right hand in His left. We stood in the old, accustomed way of not touching when one dances a waltz. We began to waltz ever so slowly. I was nervous and not quite understanding what we were doing. Jesus never said a word. He kept His gaze on my eyes and smiled, turning me as we danced. I began to note that every time He turned me, He would pull me slightly closer to Himself. Closer and closer He pulled me. My mind was asking, What is He doing? I was somewhat afraid and yet did not want to pull away or stop dancing. We turned and turned as Jesus pulled me closer and closer. All of a sudden, our faces were inches apart. I still did not know what Jesus was doing, but I knew we could not get any closer. With the next turn, Jesus pulled me into Himself, and I was no more.

Truth: "That they all may be one, as You, Father, are in Me, and I in You; that they also may be one in us, that the world may believe that You sent Me" (John 17:21).

When you come to Christ and declare by faith that He is Lord and Savior of your life, you begin your bridal stage. In the Hebrew culture, an intended groom asked the parents of a young woman for her hand in marriage. When the parents consented, the man and woman were then engaged. The man paid the parents a bridal price. This engagement was a contract and meant they were married but not living together as man and wife until a later date. This marriage contract was binding. In this stage of the engagement, the bride was to act as if married and use the time to make herself ready for the wedding day. She was to prepare her trousseau and hone her skills as a homemaker and wife as taught by her mother. Likewise, the bridegroom was to make preparation for a home for the bride. The bride was never made aware of what day her bridegroom would come. She only knew one thing. She would first hear a trumpet sound and then the wedding procession would come to her home and her bridegroom would take her away with him. They would become one together as God ordained.

> Therefore a man shall leave his father and mother and be joined to his wife, and they shall become one flesh. (Genesis 2:24)

This dream is very simple. I was the bride of Christ, and I was dressed in white because of the blood of the lamb. Christ Jesus, the sacrificial lamb, willingly laid down His life for each of us and ensures that we belong to Him. Each of us is made pure by the blood of Christ. Not by deeds, works, or faithfulness, but simply by faith in Christ Jesus as Messiah. We have been cleansed by the blood of Jesus. The wedding gown is symbolic of purity. You and I belong to Christ, and we are His bride. At the sound of the trumpet, Christ will come to receive us to Himself as His bride.

> For the Lord Himself will descend from heaven with a shout, with the voice of an archangel, and with the trumpet of God. And the dead in Christ will rise first. (1 Thessalonians 4:16)

All who are found in Christ will be clothed in white.

> He who overcomes shall be clothed in white garments, and I will not blot out his name from the Book of Life; but I will confess his name before My Father and before His angels. (Revelation 3:5)

In that day, when all has been reconciled in heaven, you will dance the wedding dance with your Lord, your ultimate bridegroom. As in the physical realm when a bride waits for her groom, you also wait and are being prepared in the spiritual realm to be presented to Christ. As you wait for the return of your bridegroom Jesus, you are to be making yourself ready for Him that you may become one with Him.

God called you to His Son. You accepted the marriage contract when you said yes to Jesus. You should then conduct yourself in the way of a wife as you wait for Jesus who has purchased you with the ultimate bridal price—His blood.

> For I am jealous for you with godly jealousy. For I have betrothed you to one husband, that I may present you as a chaste virgin to Christ. (2 Corinthians 11:2)

You are one with Christ right now as you dwell in this world. You have assurance that you belong to Him. One day He will return to bring you to your eternal home. In the interim, you are to be living as a faithful bride who longs for His return. You should have a desire for His return to come swiftly while you prepare your trousseau, which is your fruit from the years of walking with Him here on earth. You are to take great care to be true to Him, for you know not what day He will return. Once you hear the trumpet sound, you will know that your eternal union with Him is near.

When I was pulled into Jesus, I ceased to exist except only in Him. Likewise, you said the marriage vow of "I do" when you accepted Christ Jesus as Lord and Savior of your life. The symbolic picture of this is shown in following Christ in baptism after your salvation. Baptism publicly states your betrothal to Christ. In baptism, you essentially die to self as you are immersed into Him and are raised to a new life in Christ. Your engagement period started at the time of your salvation.

> Or do you not know that as many of us as were baptized into Christ Jesus were baptized into His death? Therefore we were buried with Him through baptism into death, that just as Christ was raised from the dead

by the glory of the Father, even so we also should walk in newness of life. (Romans 6:3–4)

You were clothed with Christ and now show publicly, by your behavior, actions, countenance, demeanor, that you belong to Him.

For as many of you as were baptized into Christ have put on Christ. (Galatians 3:27)

As the Hebrew bride awaited her wedding day, she was nervous, excited, wondering at how her marriage will be. When is he coming? Would she like being married? All kinds of questions and thoughts ran through her head. She, like any young girl, prepared for marriage, talked to her friends about her bridegroom, and wondered what kind of person her husband would be. She was in love.

You, as you wait for your bridegroom, Jesus, should be no different. Christ is your life, your all in all. He is the one who has purified you with His blood. Father God looks upon you as white as snow because of Christ's payment of the bridal price. Jesus lets you know how much He loves you and wants you. Are you excited as you await that day? Are you expectant of His return? Do you look for Him daily?

What a day of rejoicing that will be! What a time you shall have when your eyes see your bridegroom, who has eyes only for you, His bride. You will sit at the banqueting table of love with your Lord of lords and King of kings.

He brought me to the banqueting house, and his banner over me was love. (Song of Songs 2:4)

As in every wedding, there is a bridal dance. Usually, the bride and groom step out onto the floor alone while all others watch. This is their dance and no one else's. They have chosen a special song that speaks of their hearts. As they dance together, they declare their love to one another in song.

I am my beloved's, and my beloved is mine. (Song of Songs 6:3)

Are you ready for the wedding dance with your Lord and Savior? As the bridegroom, He is preparing a place for you that He may come again and bring you to live with Him forever.

> In My Father's house are many mansions; if it were not so, I would have told you. I go to prepare a place for you. And if I go and prepare a place for you, I will come again and receive you to Myself; that where I am, there you may be also. (John 14:2-3)

Father God declared His love for you by giving His one and only Son as the price for your sin. Jesus declared His love for you by willingly taking the cross in your place. He is a worthy bridegroom.

> Yes, I have loved you with an everlasting love; Therefore with lovingkindness I have drawn you. (Jeremiah 31:3)

Will you be found faithful when He comes for you? Will you declare your love for Him as you await His coming?

> I will declare Your name to My brethren; in the midst of the assembly I will praise You. (Psalm 22:22)

What about you?
1. Are you prepared for your wedding day with Christ? If not, what will you do to ensure you are ready?
2. Is your faithfulness to Christ evident in your walk with Him? If not, how will you resolve that?
3. Do you appreciate our Lord's love for you? If not, what will you do in order to show Him how much you value it?

SECTION VII
LOVE REVISITED

Grace, then, is grace,—that is to say, it is sovereign, it is free, it is sure, it is unconditional, and it is everlasting.
—Alexander Whyte, author

CHAPTER 20
♥ AMAZING GRACE

Amazing Grace, how sweet the sound,
That saved a wretch like me.
I once was lost but now am found,
Was blind, but now I see.

T'was Grace that taught my heart to fear.
And Grace, my fears relieved.
How precious did that Grace appear
The hour I first believed.

Through many dangers, toils, and snares
I have already come;
'Tis Grace that brought me safe thus far
and Grace will lead me home.

The Lord has promised good to me.
His word my hope secures.
He will my shield and portion be,
As long as life endures.

When we've been here ten thousand years
Bright shining as the sun.
We've no less days to sing God's praise
Than when we've first begun.

—John Newton (1725–1807)

The story of John Newton is the story of you and me. It is an amazing grace poured out of the heart of God for all of His creation; the love of a holy, sovereign God for children who are rebellious, stubborn, hard-hearted, hard-headed, and steeped in selfish desires. Yet, He loves you just as He loved John Newton as He looked upon the soul of a man in pain and darkness who needed His touch. Father God will go to great lengths to save one soul. That is seen in His giving of His Son.

John Newton, born a sinner on July 24, 1725, died a child of God on December 21, 1807. Newton was an English sailor who learned to love drink and women. He sailed ships to Africa and delved into the popular, money-making adventure of slave trading. In 1748, Newton experienced a spiritual conversion. In 1754, he gave up active slave trading, and in 1755, became an evangelical lay minister. It was not until 1788 (thirty-four years later) that Newton issued a written apology for slave trading. In his apology, he confessed the atrocities in which he participated. In 1767, Newton collaborated with William Cowper in writing a volume of hymns, including "Amazing Grace." Some of Newton's other hymns are:

"Glorious Things of Thee are Spoken," "How Sweet the Name of Jesus Sounds!" "Let Us Love, and Sing, and Wonder," "Come, My Soul, Thy Suit Prepare," and "Approach, My Soul, the Mercy-Seat."

Can you see yourself in Newton's story? He was born a sinner as all are; saved by God, continued in slave trading for a season, stopped slave trading, became a minister of the gospel of Jesus Christ, and publicly acknowledged and confessed the sin of slave trading thirty-four years after his conversion. I am reminded of my own salvation experience and my continuing in sin. God does not save you and make you perfect. It is a conversion of the heart and soul, not of the mind. You battle the flesh every step of the way. Your salvation experience is real. However, you must begin to learn the ways of your new Master and Lord. Being led by the Spirit is not an automatic privilege. It is learned. Revelation of the Word is not just dropped into your mind at the time of conversion; you need to study. In your salvation experience you are introduced to and embrace Christ Jesus as your Savior. Now you must learn about Him and grow into Him. This is why Jesus "became sin for you." You are a sinner.

> For all have sinned and fall short of the glory of God. (Romans 3:23)

By faith (the same faith Abraham possessed when he believed God) in what Jesus accomplished on the cross for you and by His blood, you are forgiven of your sins. You receive Jesus as Lord and Savior. You know you are prone to fail and even when you do, you confess your sin, are forgiven, and are brought back into the fold. I understand Newton's failure to recognize slavery as sin because his spirit had not been educated yet. He was learning as he walked with Christ as you are. Once his spirit man was convicted of the horror of slavery, he renounced it and was renewed in his spirit man. We are renewed every day.

> Therefore we do not lose heart. Even though our outward man is perishing, yet the inward man is being renewed day by day. (2 Corinthians 4:16)

How about you? Are you saved? Do you know Jesus Christ as your Lord and Savior? Are you enjoying a personal relationship with him? Do you still sin? Ah, that is the question is it not? Do you still sin after having met and embraced Christ Jesus as your Savior? If you are truthful you will answer, "Yes, I do." John Newton's story is a story of you and me. You can see in his story the love of God. God's patience is not like ours. He was willing to spend years shaping and molding this man to the image He desired Newton to be. It is not a shallow, touchy-feely love, but a lasting love that permeates every part of your being. God looked not on the outward workings of Newton but on his heart. The love of God so entrenched itself in Newton's soul it inspired some of the greatest hymns written. "Amazing Grace, how sweet the sound. . . ." It is the heart God looks on, not the outward appearance of a man. What is in your heart? Can you hear the sweet sound of grace?

Earlier we read God's words about King David:

> I have found David the son of Jesse, a man after My own heart, who will do all My will. (Acts 13:22)

God chose and anointed David when he was a seventeen-year-old boy who knew nothing but tending his father's sheep. Oh, he did know one other thing. He knew God. His days, besides keeping a watchful eye over his father's sheep, consisted of playing his harp and singing about and to God. Like Newton, David was also a songwriter. Many of David's songs are what we know as the book of Psalms. David's keeping of the sheep was training for his future kingship over the people of Israel. How was David trained? He fought bears and lions and put his life on the line for his father's sheep every single day and night. He slept with the sheep at night, refusing to let fear keep him from accomplishing his task. Though to man's eye, keeping sheep was one of the lowliest jobs one could do, David did it with all his might, all his strength, and all his love. It was the job given him by his father, and he did it well and with love.

What training is God putting you through today? Are there troubles in your life? Do you seem to always be in a spiritual fight? These times are to train you to be able to stand fast in faith and trust in God. If you are vigilant in your walk, one day you will find yourself in a higher position. God cannot place you in a higher position unless you are strong enough to handle the job. Do not despise the training you are given. It is for your good and for His glory.

David loved and worshipped God. As far as David knew, all he would ever be was a lowly shepherd. But God had other plans for David. He would be king and thus the keeper of God's sheep, Israel. In like manner, God has plans for you. He sees the person He formed you to be in your mother's womb and planned all your days before there was one of them.

> My frame was not hidden from You, when I was made in secret, and skillfully wrought in the lowest parts of the earth. Your eyes saw my substance, being yet unformed. And in Your book they all were written, The days fashioned for me, When as yet there were none of them. (Psalm 139:15-16)

The dilemma you may face today is in learning how to do the job at hand with a willing and obedient heart before He can accomplish that which He has prepared for you.

> If you are willing and obedient, you shall eat the good of the land. (Isaiah 1:19)

You must stay the course of the training you are in, trusting God all the way. Too often a person is able to envision the prize at the end of their path and they run into it ill-equipped to handle it. Many in ministry today have made this mistake. They are told by others they should preach, sing, and teach, and they step out on man's word, ahead of God. Pride and arrogance have never been good leaders. You must allow the Holy Spirit to be your teacher and learn to be led by the Spirit, trusting God with your life. You might say, "But you don't know what I am going through." You are right, I don't. But God does. Whatever it is, He has allowed it for a reason. You can trust Him to keep you and bring you through any circumstance that may be adverse to you.

David knew God. Like Newton, David too did not always walk in the right ways. Before becoming king, he endured King Saul's wrath and jealousy and ran for his life for many years. In that time, David had two opportunities to kill Saul but he did not. He told his men that Saul was God's anointed and he had no right to take his life—even though Saul was trying to take his (see 1 Samuel 24:4-10). This was an admirable trait in David. In time, Saul died and David was crowned king and reigned mightily. However, when David was older and "at the time when kings go to battle" (2 Samuel 11:1), David decided on his own to stay home. Big mistake! It was then he entered into an act of adultery. If David had been where he was supposed to be at the time (in battle) this would not have happened. Have you fallen into trouble because you were not where you were supposed to be? You thought you could handle the situation and found you could not. Can you see that much of your "stepping out" of God's will is a deliberate act of your will? You know the temptation, the danger, and you are drawn by your own lust to seek it out.

> But each one is tempted when he is drawn away by his own desires and enticed. (James 1:14)

If Satan knows what tempts you, should you not heed the warning of God rather than foolishly thinking, "I can handle this." God, in His love and compassion for you, gives you ample warning. However, many times in your yearning to satisfy the flesh, you ignore His warnings. Is it any wonder Satan knows what button to push? If you don't like apples, he will present you with oranges or grapes or whatever it is that entices you most. You must be diligent at all times to God's leading.

> Therefore, beloved, looking forward to these things, be diligent to be found by Him in peace, without spot and blameless. (2 Peter 3:14)

David's complacency caused a temptation that he was unable (or did not want) to avoid. He was led by the lust of his flesh, lust of his eyes, and pride of life.

> For all that is in the world—the lust of the flesh, the lust of the eyes, and the pride of life—is not of the Father but is of the world. (1 John 2:16)

In 2 Samuel chapters 11 and 12, we read that David's act of adultery led to Bathsheba's pregnancy. What followed was lying, deceit, and a cover-up, with all the palace guards and servants having knowledge of David's sin. Then, there was the murder of Uriah, Bathsheba's husband and a soldier in the army who had been loyal and faithful to David. The end result was the death of the baby born of this sinful union. A simple day began with David deciding not to go with his men when he should have, and it ended with the ruination of many lives—not only David's, but the lives of Bathsheba, Uriah, the illegitimate child, and David's sons and his people. Later in life David wrote the following words speaking of the revelation he learned about himself, which should reveal our own selves to us as well, and that God was ever present with him.

> I was so foolish and ignorant; I was like a beast before You. Nevertheless I am continually with You; You hold me by my right hand. (Psalm 73:22-23)

God forgave David as He did John Newton and as He has forgiven you and me. You are not perfect in your walk with Jesus. Yet, even when you fail, you keep striving to walk with Him, and He loves you all the way as your heart yearns for Him.

Whether a King David or a John Newton, we are all sinners saved by grace. You are saved by the love of a God who would not let you go, and what an amazing grace it is. Because you are covered by the blood of Christ, God looks upon you as holy, righteous, and pure. Forgiven! In His Father's heart of love, God calls you His own.

> Behold what manner of love the Father has bestowed on us, that we should be called children of God. (1 John 3:1)

Only an amazing God can love with this kind of grace. There is no place His love cannot reach you. No mountain too high, no valley so low, nor ocean too deep, that His love cannot hold you and keep you.

> For I am persuaded that neither death nor life, nor angels nor principalities nor powers, nor things present nor things to come, nor height nor depth, nor any other created thing, shall be able to separate us from the love of God which is in Christ Jesus our Lord. (Romans 8:38-39)

Amazing grace—how sweet the sound. Can you hear God's whispers of grace in your heart? Do you know this love? He knows you. He has poured His love and grace over you with such intensity that there are not enough words to describe or speak it in all of its truth. God's love is infinite, and it is for you.

What about you?
1. Do you understand and embrace the grace of God? What will you do to make sure this grace is part of your life?
2. Have you ever walked in such darkness as John Newton? What brought about a change?
3. Were you tempted to do something because of complacency in your walk with Christ? What did it cost you?

To every toiling, heavy-laden sinner, Jesus says, come to Me and rest. But there are many toiling, heavy-laden believers, too. For them this same invitation is meant. Note well the words of Jesus, if you are heavy-laden with your service, and do not mistake it. It is not, go, labor on, as perhaps you imagine. On the contrary, it is stop, turn back, come to Me and rest. Never, never did Christ send a heavy laden one to work; never, never did He send a hungry one, a weary one, a sick or sorrowing one, away on any service. For such the Bible only says, Come, come, come.
—Hudson Taylor, author

CHAPTER 21

♥ A LOVE UNRIVALED: INVITATION

Throughout my walk with Jesus, I have had one special prayer that I have asked the Lord to answer. I said to Abba Father, "If I could have one thing, just one thing, I would want to be able to tell others of Your love." I pray that as you have read this book you have seen and embraced the love of your Abba Father and of your Lord and Savior Jesus, that you have come to a greater understanding of who God is, the love He has for you in giving His own Son for you, and how much He wants you to know His love. As a father loves a child of his own flesh and yet must discipline his child when the child errs in his ways, so too does Abba Father love you and must discipline you when you turn a rebellious heart against Him.

> You should know in your heart that as a man chastens his son, so the Lord your God chastens you. (Deuteronomy 8:5)

This discipline is to turn you back to Him that you may dwell under the safety and shelter of His mighty arms. As the psalmist stated:

> Because You have been my help, therefore in the shadow of Your wings I will rejoice. (Psalm 63:7)

> He shall cover you with His feathers, and under His wings you shall take refuge; His truth shall be your shield and buckler. (Psalm 91:4)

Discipline must come when you leave the safety of God to run after other things, just as the Israelites did so many times as they desired the world's goods, ways, and even their idols. Still, in your failing, floundering and stumbling, God's love for you does not wane.

God is love! (see 1 John 4:8, 16). God created you in His image. God created you in love as He is love. God called all of His creation "good." I pray that you have come to understand that no matter what you do, God loves you with unconditional love. You may spurn Him, reject Him, but His love still stands. It is not Abba Father's desire that anyone should perish.

> The Lord is not slack concerning His promise, as some count slackness, but is longsuffering toward us, not willing that any should perish but that all should come to repentance. (2 Peter 3:9)

God's love for you is ever-present. God is patient, and He is not in a hurry to bring this world to completion. You are given time to come to know Him, to receive Christ Jesus as Lord and Savior, or to repent from falling away. However, God will not force you to love Him in return. It is His heart's desire that you know how much you are loved by the gift of His Son for you, by His actions toward you, and by His patience in waiting for you.

In the story of the prodigal son (see Luke 15), the father patiently waited for his son's return, this son who spurned him, demanded his inheritance and left home. This father waited and watched the road every day for his son to come to his senses (repent) and return home. Do you have a prodigal child? Maybe you are the prodigal child? Prayer with love can bring you home. This father's love and patience won out. One day the father saw his son, yet a long distance away down the road, coming home. The father took off running toward his son. He did not wait with a proud, pompous attitude for his son to come to him. This father ran to his son—the same son who spurned him, turned his back on him, demanded money, and left. The most important thing he wanted his son to know was how much he loved him, that he had been watching and waiting for him to come home and that he had forgiven him. Before the son could speak a word, the father's actions spoke loudly. After all he did and said to his father, he was loved. He was forgiven. His father had been watching for him. What an awesome display of love and forgiveness.

You may have heard the phrase, "What you do speaks so loudly I cannot hear what you say." The father could have waited for the son to walk all the way up the road, hanging his head in shame, fearing rejection or punishment, groveling at his feet. But the father did not. In like manner, God knows your heart. He knows you are prone to fall and when you do He is right there waiting, watching for your repentant heart to turn back to Him, waiting to hear you call, "Abba Father" that He may run and pick you up, loving you back to Himself.

This is our Father God. This is Abba Father's heart for you. As in all things you have a choice. You choose God's love, He who created you, or you reject Him for that which will never satisfy. Love is within you. Being created in God's image (God is love) and having the breath of life breathed into you, love abides in you. Throughout your life, that love is either watered by light and truth and it grows or it is squashed by life's circumstances and becomes stagnant. Every man, woman, and child seeks the fulfillment of this love. Too often it is sought in the wrong places. You may seek love not knowing exactly what it is you seek. In Psalm 139, you learned that God purposed you before you were born. His love had you in mind before birth.

All of your days were purposed to walk before Him in love before the foundation of the world.

> Blessed be the God and Father of our Lord Jesus Christ, who has blessed us with every spiritual blessing in the heavenly places in Christ, just as He chose us in Him before the foundation of the world, that we should be holy and without blame before Him in love, having predestined us to adoption as sons by Jesus Christ to Himself, according to the good pleasure of His will, to the praise of the glory of His grace, by which He made us accepted in the Beloved. (Ephesians 1:3-6)

Until you know and understand the depth of God's love for you, you will always seek something or someone to satisfy that desire for love. I pray that today you will believe God and allow His love to wash over you, fill you, and bring you into an intimate relationship with Himself. Choose to want Him and accept His gift of love through His Son Jesus. There is well-known Bible verse that most everyone knows even if they are not versed in the Bible very well.

> For God so loved the world that He gave His only begotten Son, that whoever believes in Him should not perish but have everlasting life. (John 3:16)

Note the first part: "For God so loved the world." In these six words lies a clue to the magnitude of God's love and one which many overlook: the two-letter word "so." "God *so* loved…" It does not say God loved the world, but God *so* loved the world. What is the difference? It is this. If I say, "I love you," you would accept that as my love for you, or a gesture of saying how I feel about you. You may respond, "Well, you're a Christian. You are supposed to love me." However, if I say, "I soooo love you," there is an intensity in those two letters that magnify the sincere love I have for you. It is a deeper and passionate love. So it is with the love God has for you.

God could not, would not, stand by and watch His children perish without doing something about it. Thus, Jesus! God so loved you that He purposed Jesus, His only begotten Son, to become sin on your behalf, pay the price for your sin, and die your death. He raised Jesus from the dead to show you there is life after physical death. Life eternal with God! Only someone who loves you *so* much would do something to ensure you spend eternity with them. Can you see this love for you?

I pray that your spirit man, your heart of hearts, is open to God's love today; that in reading this book, you know beyond a shadow of doubt that Abba Father loves you and that Jesus took your place on that cross. Yes, when you mess up, you can expect discipline. But know that even God's discipline is His love for you so that you not stray further.

God created you in His image, in His love. Won't you choose to invite the fullness of God the Father, God the Son, and God the Holy Spirit within you today? It is God's invitation to you. Acceptance of it, by faith in Christ Jesus, begins a journey of love the likes of which you have never known.

> For it pleased the Father that in [Jesus] all the fullness should dwell, and by Him to reconcile all things to Himself, by Him, whether things on earth or things in heaven, having made peace through the blood of His cross. (Colossians 1:19–20)

Through Christ Jesus you are reconciled to God. Only through Jesus can you even know God and know this love (John 14:6). God says that in Christ you are complete.

> For in Him dwells all the fullness of the Godhead bodily; and you are complete in Him, who is the head of all principality and power. (Colossians 2:9–10)

A deep, intimate love awaits you today. Jesus holds His hand out to you just as He did to me in many dreams and visions. You don't have to be a dreamer of dreams to dwell in the secret place with God and enjoy His presence. This is His will for you. Did you know that Scripture declares God rejoices with singing over you?

> The Lord your God in your midst, the Mighty One, will save; He will rejoice over you with gladness, He will quiet you with His love, He will rejoice over you with singing. (Zephaniah 3:17)

As you abide with Him, listen carefully. Allow His love to quiet your soul. You will know beyond a shadow of doubt that His love for you is a love unrivaled.

♥ WHEN THE NIGHT IS FALLING

Dennis Jernigan
When the night is falling
And the day is done,
I can hear you calling, "Come."
And I will come
While you sing over me.

When the night surrounds me,
All my dreams undone,
I can hear you calling, "Come."
And I will come
While you sing over me.

When the night would hide my way,
I will listen until
I hear you say:

"How I love you, child, I love you.
How I love you, child, I love you.
How I love you!

How I love you, child, I love you.
How I love you, child, I love you.
How I love you!"

When this life is over
And the race is done,
I will hear you calling, "Come."
I will come
While you sing over me.

What about you?
1. Have you accepted God's love for you?
2. Will you trust Father God with your heart today?
3. Will you invite Father God to sing over you, His child?

♥ CLOSING PRAYER

By now you should have some idea of the vast love of God for you, to what lengths He has gone and will go to ensure you spend eternity with Him, and how much He desires an intimate relationship with you. There is nothing more He can do to help you understand you are loved. Out of love, God gave His Son to pay your sin debt. Jesus willingly took your place on the cross, your punishment, because He loves you. The Holy Spirit woos you to Father God that you may know Him and be rooted in love through Christ Jesus.

As I shared in the beginning, I had great need of this love. I needed to know and be assured of God's love in my own life. God made Himself available to me that I might know Him. He stands ready to make Himself available to you as well. Won't you embrace God's love today? Everything He has done was with you in mind.

I pray for you, the reader, to know God's love as He has revealed throughout this book and that not one day will go by that you do not fully sense His presence with you and His love for you. I ask Father God:

- To take your past failings and throw them into an abyss that nothing will hinder your relationship with Him.
- That God reveal to you through His Word—Jesus is the living Word—so that you know you belong to Him no matter how many times you fail.
- That Father God will hold you tightly so that you may trust His love and know that He will never leave you nor forsake you.
- That His love allows you to experience the joy, freedom, and peace He alone gives so that you will become as a flower that blossoms into full bloom.
- That from this day forward you will never again experience conditional love and are set free to fully love God with all your being.

Thank Abba Father for the freedom you have in Christ because of His love for you. And thank Him for His continued work in making your heart like His.

For God so loves you!

♥ BIBLIOGRAPHY

Goll, Jim W., *The Seer.* (Shippensburg, Pa.: Destiny Image Publishers, 2004).
Jernigan, Dennis. *When the Night is Falling.* (*The Dennis Jernigan Collection: vol. 1.:* Shepherd's Heart Music, Inc., 1996).
Smith, Alice, *Beyond the Veil.* (Ventura, Ca.: Regal Books, 1996).
Wigglesworth, Smith, *Smith Wigglesworth Devotional.* (New Kensington, Pa.: Whitaker House, 1999).

♥ SECOND CHANCES

I believe there are many people today who have allowed past failures and mistakes to influence them to keep you from embracing God's love and forgiveness. Guilt, shame, and condemnation are heaped on your head by memories dredged up by not only Satan, but by people who love to point the finger and remind you of your failure. It is sad how many people believe they are entitled to throw that first stone. If my life story can help one person understand the love God has for them and His eagerness to forgive them, it is worth my journey. I heard something said one time that holds true: "God does not call you to minister in an area you have not walked." If you lost a child to death, I could not identify with you as strongly as someone else who has walked that road. However, I can identify with those who have failed, fallen, and feel they cannot be forgiven. You are forgiven. You can start over.

That is what this book is about: A love that invites you to start again; to have a second chance. When you come to the full realization that Jesus died for you because He knew you could not live perfectly and because you do and will sin, then you will be free to accept your Father's love as His arms are ever open to embrace you. Freedom awaits those who desire to be set free.

The Author's Story

I was saved on September 5, 1973. I attended an evangelistic crusade where I heard an evangelist speak of Jesus and His atonement for my sins. My spiritual upbringing was in the Catholic Church. However, I had begun to attend church with my then-husband. Our church at that time supported this crusade, and it was where my walk with Christ began. Though I had been taught the basic elements of Christianity, I had no personal relationship with God or Jesus. This is what I heard and desired.

When Jesus was presented that September night I saw a living Jesus, one who loved me and gave his life for me that I may spend eternity with Him. I saw a Jesus willing to forgive and not throw stones; a Jesus who embraced all of humanity and not just one certain type of people. I had not heard anyone present Jesus this way before. My spiritual eyes and ears were opened, and I saw this Jesus who was presented and felt the truth deep within my soul. I walked down the aisle and accepted Jesus Christ as my Lord and Savior.

I would like to say that my life was a bed of roses from that day forward; however, it was not. I started out with Christ, loving Him, writing poems to Him, praying, singing to Him. I tried to talk to my husband, pastor, and others but found no spiritual food to help my growth in Christ. I was exuberant in my new faith, but no one seemed to understand how I felt. I went to different churches thinking I would hear preaching similar to what I heard from the evangelist, but to no avail. It simply was not available.

After some time of being unable to find what I was seeking, as well as lack of discipleship and understanding of my newfound faith, either in the church or at home, my enthusiasm waned; not my belief in Christ Jesus, but my first love and joy in seeking for more of Him. Due to my immaturity of life in general, outside influences, as well as lack of spiritual grounding, understanding, and growth therein, I became unhappy in my marriage. I had three children and my husband was a good man and a hard worker. However, the affection I craved was not present. It seemed that what I thought I needed was always just out of reach, and yet I could not identify what it was that I sought. I wanted the love, joy, and peace I experienced when I was first saved. I felt as if I had been given a glimpse into something wonderful and then the door was shut in my face.

With the lack of discipleship and teaching of the Word of God, I began to look to the world for my needs. My years of missteps, blatant rebellion, and lack of wisdom and maturity resulted in wrong choices: the breaking of my marriage vows, which ended in a failed marriage, and running from God and yet never completely away from Him. I floundered and found myself on a path of self-destruction. Through no fault of anyone else, I entered into a lifestyle that tore apart my marriage and damaged my sons, two of whom I became estranged from because of my actions and the divorce. I take full responsibility and blame for my circumstances.

I spent five years in the secular world trying to find where I belonged, all the while living for myself and not for God. I had not forgotten God, but I did not know how to live for Him. One day, after five years, I came to my senses, saw myself as God saw me, and asked God to forgive me. To my surprise, God was there in that moment. I not only knew He was there, I felt His presence. With awe and humility, I realized He had never left me.

I was reminded of the story Jesus told of the prodigal son (Luke 15:11-32). This prodigal son had left home in shame in disgrace, spurning his father's shelter, went out and tasted of the world's offerings, became desolate, and finally was as low as a person could get. Today, he would be called a homeless man living on the streets. This son "came to his senses" about what he had done to his father and to God and why he ended up desolate. He turned to go home. Jesus told how this son's father waited and watched every day hoping and praying that his son would return to him. One day, the father saw his son coming down the road. He ran to his son and embraced him with love, tears, and forgiveness. This is God's love.

As I turned back to God, He was there waiting for me. I knew without a doubt that God forgave me. Now for the hard part—I had to forgive myself. I lived with shame, guilt, and condemnation for many years. I felt I deserved all the bad I could get and did not question it. It was my lot in life for my actions of sin. How quick we are to believe a lie of Satan when we fail and especially when we know not the Word of God. God would have us confess and be cleansed quickly. Satan would keep us down forever if it were left up to him.

At this point of the revelation of God's love for me in spite of my failings, I recommitted my life to God, embraced Jesus fully, and asked for His hand and purpose in my life. I remarried in 1989, and in 1990 I started receiving dreams, visions, and words from God. God's love revealed to me in the dreams and visions in this book, as well as the many that are not written here, brought me to the things we all seek: the absolute assurance of His love, the safety of His presence, the ability to trust in Him alone, and the peace I yearned for in my spirit, soul, and body. I found Father God's love to be pure, steadfast, and forgiving, and He does not bring up your past. In fact, when true repentance (turning away from) is made, God blots your sins out of His book (see Revelation 3:5). Only someone who loves with such passion would do this for you and me.

If asked to describe myself, it would say that I have been Eve: I was tempted, believed a lie, and succumbed to temptation. I have been Abraham, believing God, stepping out in faith to follow Him, yet stumbled and gave in to a lie to protect myself. I have been David and lusted after that which was forbidden, thus wreaking havoc in other lives and bearing the consequences. I have been the woman at the well, far more dry and thirsty than I realized, living in despair and hopelessness. I have been the adulterous woman deserving of death, yet forgiven and infused by such love as never before known. I have been Peter denying my Lord and yet searching once again for Him with tears of repentance. I have been Mark, immature and turning from the ministry of Christ and yet returning again in maturity and faith. I have been Paul. I was lost and then found by Christ. I once was blind but now I see.

I venture to say that every person identifies with many of these biblical people. Why? Because God, our Creator, knows us better than we know ourselves. He said, "For all have sinned and fall short of the glory of God" (Romans 3:23). And, "As it is written: 'There is none righteous, no, not one'" (Romans 3:10). In knowing that I am prone to sin, I can cling to and believe God loves me and that He is always there for me. When I turn back to Him He forgives me and lifts me higher than I could ever lift myself. I can now turn to Him and know He is the strength of my life. He knows my coming and my going and there is nothing in me hidden from Him (Hebrews 4:13). God gave me a second chance. He picked me up, began to teach me His ways, set me before Bible teachers where I learned the Word, and I thrived on all of it.

Blessed is he whose transgression is forgiven, whose sin is covered (Psalm 32:1).

I found that God *so* loved me that not only would He not let me go, but He brought me back to Himself in a fullness that I had not known existed and where I now dwell in a love unrivaled.

Blessings in Christ Jesus,

Pat Works

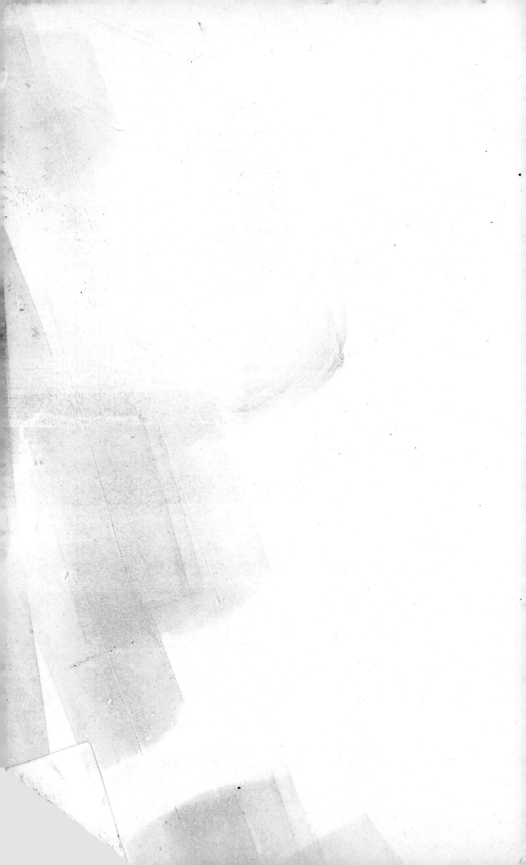

Made in the USA
Monee, IL
24 October 2021